BECOMING LILA

Praise for *Becoming Lila*

"Lila Sanden celebrates her beloved Minnesota and her time spent on the magical shores of Lake Superior. She harkens back to an America of forest cabins, aromatic trees, gleaming country lakes and plentiful wildlife. This is a celebration of family, community and the love of God and nature. Sanden's writing will lift your spirit and remind you that the world is beautiful and every day above ground is a blessing."

— *Loren Kantor, Writer and Woodcut Artist*

"Lila Sanden is a delicious writer with wonderful observational and descriptive abilities. Reading her memoir is a treat."

—*Mary Knowles, poet*

BECOMING LILA

FROM FINLAND WITH LOVE –
AN AMERICAN MEMOIR

LILA HIETALA SANDEN

ISBN: 978-1-958407-22-6 (Hardback)
ISBN: 978-1-958407-23-3 (Soft Cover)

Book design by designpanache

ELM GROVE PUBLISHING

San Antonio, Texas, USA
www.elmgrovepublishing.com

Elm Grove Publishing is a legally registered trade name of Panache Communication Arts, Inc.

CONTENTS

Sigrid from the cradle in Kajaani, she sees laundry snapping on a twine line. Feels the gentle hand rocking. Senses the snowflakes between the furrows.

— Allan Hietala

In memory
Mama, Gram, and Anna Liisa

HOW I CAME TO WRITE
MY MEMOIRS

HEARING HOW HIS great-grandmother spent a night in jail, my son Erik said, "Mom, you should write this down."

So I wrote Erik a letter:

Dear Erik,

Don't let those doll-like blue eyes fool you! Your great-grandmother was a women's libber before there were women libbers. She marched in a garment workers' union strike in protest of poor working conditions and pay, was arrested, spent the night in jail, fuming. She gave the judge a good sermon, waving her arms and wagging her finger at him. He let her go, probably in self-defense.

Once I wrote that letter, I developed an obsession. I couldn't stop writing. I had opened Fibber McGee's closet. Boxes and boxes of memories fell out, hitting me on the head. I started writing them down. Piles and piles and piles of stories spilled over my desk to the floor as the stacks grew and grew and grew into my book of memories.

In August of 2020 I received a letter:

Dear Lila,

    For years you intended to write the stories of those who loved and cared for you. But you were "too busy." I hereby give you the Gift of Time to bask in the warmth of happy times remembered and to give thanks for the bittersweet memories and the shoulders that were there for you to lean on.

    Time to write your memoirs!

THE PANDEMIC

1.

CHRISTMAS EVE, 1940

SNOW IS FALLING in Minneapolis on a bitterly cold Christmas Eve. Inside the duplex on Knox Avenue the air is filled with laughter and music. The four of us, the Hietala kids, have been bathed, shined and dressed in our Sunday outfits, thanks to big sister, Helen Joy. After Helen Joy tends to the boys, she winds my unruly hair around strips of flour sack rags. Thick brown sausage curls now encircle my head, just like Shirley Temple's! I am to be Mary in the Christmas Pageant, quite an honor for this seven year old. Gene, at five, is to sing *Silent Night*.

Earlier in the afternoon, Junior and Daddy brought in the tree, placed it in front of the bay window in the living room. Daddy had left us on our own to decorate it. As we lustily sing carols, we admire the haphazard jumble of tinsel, lots and lots of tinsel — tinsel in clumps — engulfing the crudely homemade felt and cardboard cutouts of Santa, the Baby Jesus, stars, and drums.

Mama, in her apron, lends her rich soprano voice to *Away in a Manger* as she emerges from the kitchen, where she has been cooking and baking all day in preparation for the evening's festivities. The air is filled with the warm, sweet scents of vanilla and almond mixed with the stronger aromas of nutmeg and ginger. Our noses tell us that we are soon to enjoy Mama's

Swedish meatballs and *lefse*, baked *lutefisk*, creamy mashed potatoes, gravy, beet salad and her canned carrots and green beans. Best of all, our favorite Scandinavian sweet: Norwegian rosettes.

Ah, those rosettes! Mama makes them once a year, only at Christmas. The making of them is an act of love. Each dainty star or rosette-shaped cookie is baked separately in a pot of hot oil. This requires hours of standing at the stove in order to produce enough to satisfy a crowd of appreciative fans. Mama had carried these precious jewels into the pantry, firmly instructing us not to touch them. The previous night, however, Gene and I had given in to temptation. When all was quiet, we had crawled out of our beds, shivering, as we made our way across the worn pink cabbage roses on the kitchen linoleum and on to the pantry. Our plan was to steal just one—but it is a well known fact in our family that no one eats just one rosette. No matter how careful you are, the generous dusting of powdered sugar spills over onto your clothing and the floor.

In our innocence, we thought we had gotten away with the heist. Mama must have seen the evidence we left behind, but she never said.

Now, here at the front door is Grandmother Sigrid, beaming as she presents a huge tray of her Finnish prune tarts and *Finnska Kakor* (Finnish cookies). We love our Gram, because she always beams. She is proud of our achievements. When Gram arrives for a visit, she heads straight for us kids, sits down, and gets a full report on our recent activities. Then, she lights up our world with her characteristic beam of approval.

Following her is glamorous Auntie Helvina, her brunette hair fashionably bobbed, her slim figure dressed in bright red.

The scent of *Evening in Paris* fills my lungs as she draws me close in a big hug. She has brought her Jello–a delightful mix of red Jello, canned fruit cocktail, and whipped cream. Uncle Ernie holds a squirming Lois Jane, our young cousin, in his arms. We are all eager to show her the tree.

But where is Uncle Archie, our hero? Uncle Archie is eighteen, an all-state football player. He's a tall, handsome guy with deep brown eyes that pool with tenderness when he looks at you. We are disappointed not to see him, but Gram assures us that he will come later.

It is time for our family to walk through the dark and moonless night, through the deep snow, to the Redeemer Lutheran Church. As we round the corner, we see the softly-lit stained glass windows glowing in welcome. Once in the church, Gene and I hurry off to assume our roles in the pageant. At home, I have rehearsed my silent role as Mary countless times with my dolly. Using the mirror above Mama's dresser, I have practiced the adoring maternal look I will give the Baby Jesus as I kneel beside the cradle.

I want it to be perfect.

Gene, however, didn't need to practice. Singing is as natural to him as breathing, and he never forgets the words.

The moment is here. The church is in darkness, broken only by a single bright light upon the manger. An expectant silence has fallen over the crowded pews as Joseph and I kneel beside the baby. My eyes are focusing on the baby. I am sure I have captured the look.

I am Mary.

A loud, high shriek cuts through the stillness. Tiny Lois Jane has not been fooled by my expert acting job.

"Lila Lou!" she screams. "It's Lila Looou!"

Lois Jane is leaping out of the front pew. She is flying head-long in my direction. Uncle Ernie is lunging forward to pull her back. There is a loud buzzing and muffled laughter in the pews.

My maternal look turns to an angry glare. I half-rise to shush her. But, here is Gene, unruffled, an angel in his starched white robe, stepping forward as he begins to sing *Silent Night*. There is a sudden hush as his high soprano floats through the sanctuary. All is quiet. And all is peaceful in the heart of Mary. And the families in the pews.

Back home, we gather in the living room to visit before the long-awaited supper. We kids are playing around the tree, noticing there are very few presents under it.

Will Santa come? The hard times of the depression are still with us. Our expectations are modest. We are used to creating our own amusements. Store-bought toys are a rarity in our household. But we do dream that Santa might have just one surprise in store for each of us.

Wait... Quiet... Listen! Is that the jingling of bells? We all rush to the window, to peer out as the sound gets closer. A strong wind is blowing the snow against the glass, but we see a blurry figure approaching the steps leading up to the kitchen door. He is dressed in red, has a long white beard, and is carrying a bulging potato sack.

"It's Santa Claus!" shouts Gene, Helen Joy, Allan, all the adults, and the perceptive Lois Jane.

As for me, I have quietly observed Santa's loping gait, a football player's distinctive swagger.

"It's Uncle Archie!" I yell above the hubbub.

Fortunately, my comments are dismissed by the younger

set, whose belief in Santa Claus remains unshaken. I am so glad to see Uncle Archie with that sack full of gifts, that I begin to wonder.

Maybe Uncle Archie *is* Santa Claus?

The gifts Santa-Archie brings are all we could wish for. Helen Joy models an elegant white fur hat, Junior and Gene, cowboy outfits. I am ecstatic with my very own white fur muff, just like Shirley Temple's! The older folk seem to find the rag doll I secretly made for Gene particularly amusing. Uncle Ernie's thick mustache begins to twitch upward. Everyone begins to laugh at the sight of Daisy. Daisy is my first solo attempt at sewing. Her head is attached in a most peculiar position, flat against her shoulder. Her mouth, nose, and eyes are scattered unevenly across her face. Gene falls in love with Daisy. I am proud of my efforts. Gram beams.

All too soon, the merry time together over the heavy-laden table quickly fades into the sighs of contentment that come after consuming a traditional Finnish Christmas meal. It is time to say goodbye to our guests.

Lois Jane has fallen asleep in her father's arms. Gene and I are very sleepy, but we join in the hugs and the loud chorus of goodbyes before the door at last closes on Christmas Eve 1940. Mama is tucking the blankets around our drowsy heads.

"Mama, this is the *bestest* Christmas ever," I tell her.

Mama smiles as she wishes us happy dreams.

"Don't forget that you two rascals must wait until breakfast, when, maybe, you may have just one rosette."

2.

THE HIETALA FAMILY
MUSICAL EVENING

THERE IS A PARTY atmosphere this summer Saturday morning in the Hietala family home in North Minneapolis. Helen Joy is in charge. But, for the moment, Helen Joy is deeply asleep in her half of the narrow bed she shares with me, Lila Lou, her little sister.

I have been keeping still, awake for a long time, watching the bedside clock make its slow way to eight o'clock. Whereupon, I say, "Wake up, Helen Joy! It's Saturday! Time for Jack Armstrong! And *Let's Pretend*!"

Helen Joy opens her right eye, the other eye still buried deep in the pillow. Her legs are hurting. "Go back to sleep," she mutters.

I tug at the blanket. "Get up–you promised."

Junior and Geney Boy are in their bedroom across the hall. They join in, shouting, "Jack Armstrong! We don't want to be late for Jack Armstrong!"

Now, fully awake, Helen Joy is transformed into her own sweet self. Mama tells her that the pains she feels, more and more often, are "growing pains." At thirteen, her body cannot keep up with its rapid growth. She is too thin, suddenly tall at five feet seven inches.

Helen Joy is the family baby-sitter. Mama is off for the day, working in the deli. Daddy is at his barbershop. A shave and a haircut, 35 cents. Sometimes Mama sends us to the Saturday afternoon movies. 10 cents a head. Shirley Temple is *Heidi*. Judy Garland and Mickey Rooney are on the big screen.

Helen Joy feels grown-up. Excited to be entrusted with the care of her brothers and sister. She will ignore the ache. She has plans for an evening filled with music, dance and fun. She is the creator, producer, and choreographer of the "Hietala Family Musical Evening," a regular Saturday event.

Helen Joy leaps out of bed, hugs me, and tells the boys to hurry.

The boys are dressed in cotton pants and shirts, torn here and there in the fashion of hand-me-downs. They each sport a head of bleached blond hair. The resemblance stops there. Junior's hair is carefully parted and combed. Geney Boy's stubborn hair refuses to lie down. He carries a field of straw on top of his head, spikes rising up to the heavens, giving him a look of surprise. Gene is full of fun and games, while Junior is far less impulsive.

The cereal bowls are on the table by the time we girls arrive in the kitchen. Helen Joy pours the Wheaties—"The Breakfast of Champions"—and the milk, then makes toast and opens a jar of Mama's strawberry jelly.

The dishes are washed, dried and put away. The boys are itching to get to the living room. We sit on the floor—all four of us—staring at the Philco radio. It rests in a new mahogany cabinet. Suddenly, it comes alive. Sweeps us inside with these golden words:

"Now, it's time for *The Adventures of Jack Armstrong, the All-American Boy!*"

Next, *Let's Pretend* begins its weekly trip into a fantasy world of fairies, ogres, princes and princesses. Helen Joy is glad to wander into a happy world, if even for a little while.

It is the late summer of 1942. The war against Japan and Germany has been going on for close to a year, since Japan bombed Pearl Harbor. Mama is an air raid warden, dons a helmet and patrols the neighborhood during blackout drills. The whole world goes dark. I am frightened by the darkness. Helen Joy holds me, tells me a funny story.

I am also afraid that I know something really bad that I can't share with Helen Joy or Junior or Mama because it is too scary: Daddy looks like Adolph Hitler. He has the same black hair and mustache. Could Daddy be Adolph Hitler? Going off every day to kill people and coming home at night to be a nice Daddy to his children?

The schools run air raid drills with the children. One long beep means scurry to a safe place, like the hallway or under a desk. A series of short beeps means the students should run home. Geney Boy is afraid to run home all alone, so his teacher offers to keep him safe at the school.

Linda Braun, next door, is teaching Helen Joy and me how to make candy out of potatoes. There is a flour and sugar shortage.

Everyone is worried about the fathers, sons and brothers who have gone to fight in the war. Uncle Archie is in the Pacific fighting the Japanese. Uncle Harold is in Europe fighting the Nazis. The world has become a fearful, sad place.

But Helen Joy, on this Saturday morning, has found a

way to bring light into the darkness.

She turns off the radio and ushers us down to the basement, into the windowless room by the coal chute. In schoolmarm fashion, she assigns the roles in the drama of the day. Patiently teaches songs, lines, and dance steps.

Her warm spirit flows through the basement, chases the cold and gloom away.

We enter a small storage room to find costumes among the cast-offs in an old wooden trunk. Worn curtains and sheets work well.

At 7 p.m. we are in costume, ready for The Hietala Family Musical Evening. The first act's centerpiece is the radio. Mama and Daddy sit in comfortable chairs in front of it. We children sit on the floor at their feet. Daddy turns a dial, and a voice beckons us into *This is Your Hit Parade!* The music begins. As those familiar songs of the 30s and 40s pour out, our voices fill the room. Helen Joy and Mama leading with their high sopranos.

The program is over. Daddy switches off the radio. It is time for the second act: the children's theater. Geney Boy and I perform a dance we call "The Stiff Man's Dance." Geney Boy dances around on tiptoe, leans forward, as if to lose his balance. Then, he falls backward, stiff as a board, while I stand behind to catch him just before he hits his head on the hardwood floor.

Fortunately, he never does. Mama breathes a sigh of relief.

Mama and Daddy are impressed with Junior's rendering of Gene Autry's *Back in the Saddle Again.* Helen Joy and I sing duets: Judy Garland's hit, *Somewhere Over the Rainbow* and the 1939 Western, *You Are My Sunshine.*

On these Saturday evenings, the war is forgotten.

At fifteen, Helen Joy announces that she will answer only to Helen. I adore my sister and want to be just like her. So, I, Lila Lou, shorten my name to *Lila*. Helen gets her first job at the neighborhood drugstore on Glenwood Avenue. Helen is the most beautiful soda jerk. Her dark hair shines like silk as it frames her classic features. Helen's smile reflects her loving heart. Geney Boy and I climb up, sit on the high stools at the soda fountain to enjoy our first milkshakes. Cold chocolate, creamy goodness, swirls around our tongues.

In one word, Helen is sweet. Like the milkshakes.

But behind her smile, there is the hurting, always there. Like a sharp poker awakening her at night. Wearing her out in gym class at the high school. There are some days she feels too cold, too much in pain, to go to school. She sits next to the dining room stove, wrapped in a blanket, in an effort to get comfortable. Minnesota winters are insufferable.

One day, I am home sick from school. I join Helen at the stove, see how frail she is. I don't understand the depth of her illness. Mama rarely takes us children to a doctor. But, finally, she takes Helen.

Helen is diagnosed with young onset rheumatoid arthritis. There is no cure. Now, she has received what could be a life sentence.

One which she will ignore.

Helen has every intention of enjoying her life. An artist, her work is published in the *Minneapolis Star-Tribune*—a full page pen and ink portrait of President Lincoln. She wins a scholarship to the Minneapolis Art Institute. Her portraits rival the work of a mature artist.

Helen has a beautiful lyric soprano voice. She studies at the McPhail School of Music.

We sing duets at the church. Helen is my voice teacher.

I notice that Helen is changing in many ways. She seems a different person from the one I shared a bedroom with since early childhood. She is suddenly a stranger. One who wears nylons and high heels. Bottles of perfume and cosmetics crowd the dresser. Lovely blouses, skirts, dresses and shoes appear in our tiny closet. There, beside them, hangs a shimmering blue satin evening gown that Helen wears as she sings her first recital at the music school.

"Stop breathing!" Helen shouts, angry at me for disturbing her sleep with one of my frequent hiccup attacks. She no longer spends time with me, preferring to go out with her girlfriends or the steady stream of young men who call to take her on dates.

It is a frigid winter night in Minneapolis. How graceful Helen is, as she tosses her long wavy locks, sweeps down the front hall stairs to greet her escort of the evening. Mama is there to make sure the young man understands the house rules of behavior. Rules that must be obeyed. Gram and I are there, too, having crept up to stand behind Mama. Helen's date needs to pass our inspection, too.

"Helen, did you remember to put on your long underwear?" Gram, being hard of hearing, speaks loudly, the better to hear herself. Helen turns scarlet in a mix of embarrassment and anger, while her date, squirming, appears to be backing out the door. Helen is quite annoyed at the two of us. She glares at Gram, sees me gawking up at her date from my position behind Mama.

Gram and I are forever banned from the foyer on Helen's date nights. We are forced to become co-conspirators, silently eavesdropping from around the corner in the living room.

Helen has moved into another world, leaving me behind to wait my turn. She does not like sharing a bedroom with me. We no longer talk and giggle as before.

Where has my sweet sister gone?

Helen is seated at the old vanity dresser. I am standing beside her. She is brushing her hair away from her face. I take my hairbrush to copy her. Gazing into the mirror, Helen studies her face, her bared forehead, and then mine.

"Look, Lila! My face is heart-shaped."

Smiling in self-admiration as she points to her forehead with its charming widow's peak. A perfect heart.

I think of a new word I have found in the dictionary. Could Helen have turned into a *narcissist*?

Helen turns to look at me. To my face, my forehead, to be exact. She points to the place where my forehead narrows significantly on both sides, comparing it to her lovely wideness.

Helen observes that I have a diamond-shaped face. That sounds okay to me. I can live with this. Maybe even be a little proud of what may have been the result of a difficult birth?

What she utters next causes me to take another look in the mirror.

"A pinhead! That's what you are! A pinhead!"

Pinhead—my new nickname.

I think that having to go through life with a pointed head could be a bit depressing. But being Helen's pinhead brings us close, the way we were before she started to act like a grownup.

"Hey, Pinhead!" Helen shouts. And I feel special. A

pointed head isn't so bad after all.

Helen leaves home after two years in a business college. She takes a position as a secretary for a well-known magazine. She marries Ernie, tall, handsome, and gifted with a most pleasant disposition. They raise five children. Ernie, Grant, Guy and Adam favor their father, and the girl, Cathy, her mother.

Helen feels blessed to be surrounded by the love of her family. But, as foretold by her doctors, her pain increases over the years, rendering her disabled. Her pain is great, but her love for her family is even greater. Even in the final stages of her disease, when she is losing the ability to walk, when her hands are becoming useless, she takes care of her grandchildren. She has watched over young babies and children all her life. She sings to them, makes them laugh, as she did for her brothers and sister a lifetime ago. Helen's smile masks an unrelenting, overwhelming pain.

Helen nurses Ernie during his illness and death from cancer at sixty-two.

Helen is living alone, her extensive supply of books and the Minnesota Twins, her most loved companions. She relies on family and chance visitors to help her. The day comes when she must admit to herself that she will not survive without constant help and monitoring. Her days in a nursing home bring some relief. But her disease affects her mind. Helen becomes delusional, tortured by suspicions that those who most love her are harming her. Only death will bring her solace.

I visit her in the nursing home. Helen is asleep.

"Sweet Helen Joy," I sigh. "Where have you gone?"

For the moment, Helen Joy is wholly present. She stirs, reaches out to touch me. Her eyes mist over with love for her little sister.

"Sweet Helen Joy," I croon as I reach out to kiss her.

Sometimes, years after her death, I conjure up Helen Joy, young and beautiful. I am standing before the dressing table. Helen Joy is sitting in front of me, looking into the mirror. She smiles approvingly as she smooths her wavy hair.

Helen Joy greets me.

"Hey, Pinhead!"

3.

GOODBYE GENEY BOY

My earliest memories are of my little brother, Geney Boy, dancing. His shock of golden hair falling over his face. Geney Boy is giggling and jiggling and singing as he flies over the living room floor. A happy fella! Not just happy — Geney Boy radiates exuberance. His inner joy bubbles over, washes over all our family.

Where did Gene come from? The rest of us were admittedly a bit too reserved. Too cautious. But with Gene's arrival all that changed. Gene taught us to dance freely, with abandon. To sing and laugh loudly. To giggle often.

That is not to say that sometimes a little boy, just five, can be too scared to sing. Especially when he is in the care of his seven year old sister who is scared, too.

I don't know if she just happens to be there, but there she is, an elderly lady, hair white as snow, on her front porch. Grandma Braun — as we call our next door neighbor — hums *Jesus Loves Me* while moving her wicker rocker back and forth, in perfect rhythm. She seems glad to see that Gene and I have made it safely on the walk home from school. So are we. We are afraid of getting snatched by a bad person!

But no longer. Grandma Braun's aproned lap is ample enough for two little kids. All our fears evaporate as she holds us, so calm and unhurried. She smells of cookie dough. Better yet, she has brought out a plate of warm sugar cookies, baked just for us. We bend her ear, telling her about our day at school.

Soothed and fortified, we head home. We encounter Grandpa Braun in his garden. Grandpa Braun, is tall, lean, and stern in his worn black suit. He always seems ready to attend a funeral. His steel-rimmed glasses reflect the sunlight. He whistles as he watches over the bright purple, red, pink, yellow, orange and white blossoms that border the land between our homes. He holds his gardening scissors in his hands, long sharp knives, and points them at us. Thunders, "Don't even touch these flowers! Or I'll cut off your ears!"

Then he gives us a big smile. Grandpa Braun is teasing us. This is his way of saying that he likes us. It takes us a while to understand that.

It should be comforting to know that Grandpa Braun is close by and that he likes us. But Gene and I get really scared as we approach the kitchen door to our empty house.

What if it isn't empty?

We stand at the door to gather up some courage. Two steps and we are inside the kitchen. No one is there. But is someone lurking around the corner in the dining room? Or hiding in a closet? Under the table? Gene and I begin to shout loudly.

"Mama is on the porch! She is coming in!"

"Here comes Grandpa Braun! He has big sharp scissors!"

Then we wobble, *"Here We Go Round the Mulberry Bush."*

We muster up an ounce of bravery, *"Who's Afraid of the Big Bad Wolf?"*

All quiet. We breathe. We are once more safe from robbers, gangsters and monsters.

You grow up fast when your parents have to leave you alone while they are working to provide the bare necessities. Your older brother and sister are in school all day, so you must wait for long hours for them to return home.

Looking back, I don't think that Gene ever felt safe. He was the baby in a family of hard-working achievers. How could he even begin to compete with them? Gene was a natural performer with a pure singing voice and a golden touch at the piano. But he did not believe that he had a rare gift for music. I have always sensed that Gene's lack of self-confidence had much to do with the fact that he was tiny, by far the smallest boy in his class. He did not seem to fit in with his peers, who were significantly bigger. School was not a safe place for Gene. Beneath his shy smile he kept a secret. Gene was alone and unhappy with who he was.

He was rudderless. He wandered through his school years almost unnoticed. He did not cause trouble. He was an average student. But he had no real passion.

We all worried about Gene.

Gene turned seventeen in 1952, in the midst of the Korean War. Big brother Allan enlisted in the Air Force in 1951. Gene left in the middle of his senior year in high school to serve in the Army. I believe that although patriotism was a part of his decision, Gene felt a need to prove that he, too, was a man. That he was unafraid to step out of his safety zone.

In 1953, our family received news that Gene had been wounded while serving in an artillery unit. Despite a head injury, he managed to crawl to a buddy in a futile attempt to save him. He was awarded a bronze star. He suffered brain trauma and memory loss. He returned home from Korea, a damaged soul.

Gene was afflicted with an ongoing nightmare. In the dark of night he would awaken, sobbing. Reliving over and over, the ear shattering whine of the bomb, his legs and arms paralyzed as he crawls on his belly, never to reach his friend in time to save him.

Gene was not well. He courageously earned his GED. He managed a year and a half at the University of Minnesota, but couldn't concentrate on his studies. He married, had two children, but soon divorced.

Although he was rated a number one salesman in his area, Northrup King, the world's largest seed company, had to let Gene go. Gene couldn't recall important data related to his work. His memory loss led to joblessness.

Gene was troubled and anxious. He became homeless. Unable to function on his own, he became flat and lifeless.

Ultimately, he was admitted to the VA home in Hastings, Minnesota. He lived in the care of the VA for 37 years.

Over time Gene began to thrive at the home. He entered a work therapy program. He learned how to make poppies. He liked to drink caffeine-free Diet Coke, play bingo, and shoot pool. He loved to go to the casino, and play cards—especially poker with his comrades. He took long walks through nearby parks and gardens. He spent hours birdwatching. He moved through the seasons in awe of God's creation.

Back in the 1980s, I got a phone call from Gene, excitement in his voice. My ears perked up. Gene sounded like the old Gene. The one who was always about to burst into song.

"Have you read any books by Louie L'Amour?"

Gene's world was expanding. He came alive when he read (and reread) as many of L'Amour's cowboy stories that he could get his hands on.

The old Gene emerged when he entertained his friends with a very fast version of boogie on the piano. Sang with his buddies.

The chaplain was his closest friend. Gene was a serious Bible student. They were engaged in an ongoing conversation about their Christian faith. Gene assisted her in the chapel's worship services. Always gentle and compassionate, he became more so as his faith deepened.

Gene was no longer lonely. He reached out to his buddies. Developed deep and lasting friendships. Gave himself to others. Cards from his friends covered a wall in his room.

Gene felt safe at last.

Gene passed away several years ago. Our family and Gene's friends filled the chapel to say goodbye to this quiet, gentle brother and friend. I looked at this large group of veterans, those injured souls whose bravery had scarred them for life. Here they were, Gene's other family, bound together in love and hope for one of theirs.

And I loved them, how I loved them, and wept for each of them and for Gene.

The chaplain spoke.

She cried.

Allan shared stories of Gene's love of music and his brief career in the army. His struggle to resume a normal life in the face of his injuries. I recalled the happy memories of our childhood. Little Geney Boy, so alive, singing and dancing, bringing smiles to our faces.

And we all said goodbye to the scared little boy who grew up to be a hero.

4.

CHRISTMAS AT THE
FARMHOUSE, 1943

IT WAS EARLY MORNING, 20 degrees below zero, on the day before Christmas, 1943. Overnight, snow fell, heavy and unrelenting, outside the old farmhouse, layering the window panes with a thick coat of frost. Well, actually, the Hietala home was no longer a functioning farmhouse. In the 1930s, a large farm in the north end of Minneapolis had been parceled off into small lots, and streets were laid. New, modern homes were built on all sides of the original farmhouse with city water, sewage, electricity and phone lines. Over the summer our family settled into the farmhouse, having left the rented duplex on Knox Avenue for the more spacious home on Aldrich Avenue. The fields of the farm were long gone, but the farmhouse remained unchanged except for some conveniences haphazardly installed within. Most notably, a modern toilet, sink and tub were installed in the fourth and largest bedroom, now a bathroom. Sink and toilet a long walk apart.

The front porch of the white clapboard house was inhabited by a weathered wicker rocking chair, left behind when the farmer and his wife moved to an apartment in the city. Out back, a flat grassy area, now blanketed with snow, had become a play yard for the Hietala kids. A clothesline was occupied by a number of frozen shirts, trousers, sheets and towels flapping noisily in the bitter wind. A lone apple tree, a few lilac and forsythia bushes and a fair-sized garden stood buried in the deep snow.

Mama in her faded house-dress had been in the kitchen for several hours, chopping, stirring, straining, rolling, baking. Down in the basement, at bedtime, Daddy banked the fire in the coal furnace, leaving the upper floor without heat. Helen Joy, fourteen, and I, ten years old, red-nosed and shivering, rushed down from our cold bedroom to the kitchen and some of Mama's hot oatmeal. As we entered the kitchen a burst of warm air mixed with the sweet aroma of almond told us that Mama's *Finnska Kakor*—Finnish cookies—were in the oven. These delicate cookies, along with Mama's Norwegian rosettes and Grandmother Sigrid's Finnish prune tarts were our favorite holiday treats. The melt-in-your-mouth rosettes had been baked and hidden earlier in the week.

As HJ filled our bowls, topping the steaming oatmeal with brown sugar and a pat of butter, I dashed through the unheated back storage room to retrieve the two bottles the milkman had left on the back steps. No brothers around yet, so HJ and I dipped our spoons into the frozen cream at the top of the bottle. Ice cream for breakfast! A Christmas treat.

Oops! Here come the boys! HJ hurried to get Junior and Geney Boy their oatmeal before they filled their stomachs with the cream. Mama continued to step about the kitchen carrying dishes and pots hither and yon. We sat around the table, trying to guess what might be in the boxes that had appeared in the living room, waiting to be put under the tree. The level of excitement reached a fevered pitch. Geney Boy jumped up from his chair, danced around the table, singing a less than sober version of *Silent Night*. Junior slipped his ocarina out of his pocket. He warmed up with a soulful rendering of *Home on the Range*. HJ and I raised our voices as we planned our Christmas Eve hairdos. Mine, long beribboned braids, like Dorothy's in *The Wizard of OZ*. Spooky, the black cat, who lived in fear since his stepped-on tail fell off, tried to make a run for it. He charged into the bottom of Geney Boy's foot. Geney Boy fell; cat and Geney Boy howled. Mama collided with Geney Boy. Mama spilled her bowl of batter over his face. HJ and I doubled over with laughter.

"Quiet!" Mama yelled. Mama never yelled.

We all stared at her.

Mama's frown got our full attention. Mama rarely frowned.

Mama paused. Adjusted her house-dress.

Then, Mama, ever-so-sweetly and calmly suggested that Junior and Geney Boy might want to shovel the porch, steps, and sidewalks. The air will do them good. She further suggested that they might like to go down to the pond to skate.

While the boys were out shoveling, HJ and I helped Mama roll the Swedish meatballs. Not too big, not too small. We peeled the potatoes for mashing. Mama sent me down to the basement to get a jar of her cherry conserve, a luxury jam of black cherries and pecans she had preserved during canning season in the summer. I also brought up several jars of green beans, peaches and pears.

HJ and I were sent into the dining room to add a final polishing to the old oak table and sideboard. We carefully placed the plates, forks, knives and spoons in their proper places. We were well-drilled in setting the table. This was our task every Sunday after church when the family gathered for noon dinner, most always a baked chicken, potatoes and green vegetables, followed by cake or pie. Our favorite dessert was lemon meringue or banana cream pie—if we had bananas—scarce in the Minnesota winter.

It was now afternoon. We girls sat down to sample some deviled eggs, coffee for Mama and hot chocolate for HJ and me. The boys came through the kitchen door, shaking snow all over the linoleum. There was just enough time to dry their jackets and boots over the heating vents before they needed to go out to clear a path for our company. With just one bathroom, one tub, for all the family, we had to start early to dress for the evening. Daddy would soon arrive home from his barbershop, with him the Christmas tree. We had to be ready to decorate it, get it done before the church service and the arrival of Gram, Auntie Helvina—with her red Jello, fruit and whipped cream—Uncle Ernie, and young cousins Lois Jane and Jimmy. Cousin Sadie, single and alone in the city, would be with us. Cousin Matt, a Navy pilot, would be here. Soon he would leave to join his brother, our cousin Sanfrid, also a Navy pilot, to fight the war against Japan. Uncle Archie was somewhere in the Pacific with the Navy Seabees. Uncle Harold with the army somewhere in Europe.

Things started to happen fast. Daddy, his mustache and eyebrows coated with frost, came into the front hall with the tree. We all rushed to help him get the tree into the living room, where he and Mama left us kids to hang the brightly colored globes, tired homemade angels, Santas and tinsel. HJ carefully straightened, pressed and hung each shiny strand, one at a time, but her efforts were lost in the bunches that the boys and I heaped on the tree. We sang carols as we worked. HJ and I harmonized on a duet we had performed for the Ladies Aid Society — *The Birthday of a King*. Daddy joined us with his clarinet. Mama played chords on the piano.

Seven p.m. at the red brick Salem Swedish Evangelical Lutheran Church. A short walk from the farmhouse through a sharp wind and drifting snow. The congregation was packed into the pews. The smell of wet woolen was tempered by the warmth of candlelight. Our family filled two pews. I went off to join the junior choir. Down front, Bess Olson was at the organ playing a prelude from Handel's *Messiah*. The service was about to begin. The church was dark, except for the dim glow of the candles.

Bess began a triumphant arrangement of *O Come, All Ye Faithful*. Pastor Reuben Anderson, followed by the junior and senior choirs, splendid in white surplices and black skirts, processed down the center aisle.

That is, all except me. A wave of anxiety moved through me. I left the procession, scooted up the steep wooden steps to the darkened balcony at the back of the church. Where I was to sing my first solo.

Even now, after a lifetime, I find myself reliving the moment I entered the balcony:

The darkness hits me like a thud. It is pitch black up here. I am all alone in the dark! My heart racing, my stomach churning, as I grope through the darkness for the railing. Looking down — oh, how far down they are — I see the tops of the heads of over 300 people. All those ladies hats, bright reds and greens, white and brown furs, all those bald and shining heads of the men, waiting for me to sing! And I am not sure I can find my voice. It is stuck somewhere deep down inside me. My head is swimming. I entertain thoughts of fainting and falling over the railing, down, down, to land on one of those bald heads.

Then, as I look down at the choir, so distant, so far below, I see Mrs. Anderson, the pastor's wife and choir director, looking up at me, her radiant smile a brilliant light in the soft candlelight of the sanctuary. White-haired Bess Olson swings around on the organ bench with a big smile, sends yet another shaft of light up and over the pews. Straight to my heart.

My fear evaporates. My legs stop shaking. My heart stops racing. I sing with all my being to the beaming Mrs. Anderson, to Bess Olson, to all the hats and heads of the people in the pews. I sing the good news:

"Go, tell it on the mountain,
Over the hills and everywhere,
Go tell it on the mountain,
That Jesus Christ is born!"

Later, at the farmhouse, our family gathered in love to feast on traditional Scandinavian food. To be thankful for the many gifts that were given and received. Some seen, some unseen. Gram had knit colorful wool scarves to keep us warm in the harsh Minnesota winter. The lemon yellow chenille robe that cousin Sadie gave me is to be forever remembered, since it was my first robe, and dear Sadie sacrificed greatly to give it. The remembrance of Mama working in her kitchen, all the while teaching her children, as Jesus did, how to love, will forever fill my soul with gratitude. Daddy is still banking the furnace and bringing in the Christmas tree. Junior is playing a cowboy song on his sweet potato while Geney Boy dances around the kitchen. HJ and I are singing duets while she braids my hair, just like Dorothy's. Gram is still knitting, each stitch a work of love. Auntie Helvina is serving up her Jello dish. Uncle Ernie and the cousins—Lois Jane, Jimmy, Matt and Sadie—forever smiling, loving and being loved. Cousin Sanfrid, Uncle Archie, and Uncle Harold, away in the war, always present in my heart.

Mrs. Anderson, the pastor's wife, and Bess Olson, the organist, are forever there in the church on Christmas Eve 1943, looking up, smiling in approval at a little girl, ten, who is about to sing her first solo.

Sing Noel!

5.

AN UPSIDE-DOWN
WORLD

1945. MAMA IS AT the stove stirring a pot of stew. We four children gather around the kitchen table. Junior reaches into his pocket for his ocarina. He calls it his "Sweet Potato." Junior likes to share some of his favorite cowboy songs while we wait for our supper. He plays a haunting melody, his true, strong voice singing the heart-rending *Song of the Blind. Friends, I cannot see my way…*

Junior has chosen a sad song, rather than one of the light-hearted ones he routinely sings.

"I'm not hungry, Mama," Junior says. "I think I'll go up to my room to study."

Mama insists he stay at the table. He will love her stew.

Mama doesn't know that Junior has begun to dread sitting down at the table to eat dinner with our family. Daddy sits so quiet, thinking his own thoughts. He scarcely looks at his children. Shows no interest in them. Or in Mama. Daddy would rather be somewhere else.

"Daddy lives in his own world," Junior thinks. "And we are not a part of it."

Daddy's silence is fearful. Junior thinks it is like a poison that floats through the air, across the table. We all breathe it in.

We are afraid. Something bad is about to happen. Our throats tighten, swell, and none of us speak.

There is a terrible quiet at the table. The clinking of forks and spoons resonates in the silence. It is a sad, lonely sound.

Later, in the middle of the night, Junior lies in his bed, awake. He hears Daddy stumbling as he climbs the stairs to his bedroom. Catches the scent of whisky.

Junior and I live in a troubled world. Junior and I, at fourteen and twelve, are close. We do not share our fear—our sadness—about our family. To speak of it makes it worse. Junior, perhaps subconsciously, begins to create another world. It is our private world, just for the two of us. One in which we smile and laugh. Junior has a gift for turning a bad situation into a tolerable one.

When your world turns upside down, you can leave it for another.

Arriving home from school to an empty house, Junior becomes the character of the day. He bursts through the door, an extremely bow-legged cowboy. He is out on the lone prairie, dragging his horse, Sleepy, who is asleep on his feet and refuses to budge. Or, Junior is a gangster straight out of 1920s Chicago. Or he is Boris Karloff as a mad scientist.

Or—my favorite—a creature of his own invention, Oswald. Oswald is an ancient, wizened man, a self-proclaimed genius, who becomes my egocentric mentor.

"Child!" Oswald summons me in his dry, creaky voice. Junior's face is a shriveled up road map of wrinkles.

"If'n you want to attain fame as the world's smartest woman, a genius, like me, you need to eat your Wheaties. A box in the morning, a box at noon, a box before bed and you need to set your alarm for a box at 3 a.m. You must chew each mouthful 100 times. Only then will you find your mind expanding, blossoming into a rare flower that contains the secrets of the universe."

Our after school visits to Junior's imaginary world are like a salve on a wound. For a while we are normal, happy kids living in a normal, happy home.

* * *

1939. Our backyard may have a few leaves of grass, but I don't see them. It is all dirt. Dirt pounded down hard by a gang of neighborhood boys and one undersized tomboy, me. It is Saturday afternoon, time for the weekly games led by Junior. 10 noisy boys in high spirits are gathering. They are ready to get some exercise after a morning spent listening to the Saturday morning radio shows.

Before Junior divides the boys into teams, he tells me to go play with my girlfriends.

"These are boys' games. Rough. You might get hurt," he warns.

"I'm as good as any boy," I boast. Junior is no match for his stubborn sister.

We are playing "Kick the Can." Kicking an empty food can over the garage roof. All of us run around to tag the boy who catches it, before he rounds the corner to the opposite side of the garage. No one gets hurt in this game, although one of the boys cries out in pain when the can hits him on the head.

Junior takes us to our neighbor's yard. It is covered in grass, Junior explains, soft and safe for when we fall down in the next game, "Crack the Whip." He lines us up in a row. Instructs us to hold hands. We are the whip. The object is to run as fast as we can, holding on tight to our left and right neighbors' hands. When the leader stops suddenly, we will all jerk to a stop and fall into a pile on the lawn.

"Fun!" everyone shouts.

What Junior doesn't say is that the person on the end of the whip is thrown through the air if she happens to be a tiny little girl with a weak grip. Junior also doesn't notice the nearby concrete stairs. The next thing I know I'm airborne, my head bouncing off the corners of our neighbor's concrete steps.

Junior feels responsible. He is my protector.

"It's not your fault," I tell him, as Mama wraps a towel around my bloody head, and carries me off to the doctor.

Junior lets me play ball with the boys. He thinks this should be safe for his little sister. He doesn't expect that I will kick off my too tight shoes and run barefoot over a trail of broken glass while chasing the ball.

Mama has to carry me to the doctor's so often that he finally tells her to keep me home with my dolly.

In seventh grade, Junior drops his nickname. He is now Allan. He begins to train for the high school gymnastics team. His work ethic is sterling. He excels in all events. As a high school senior, he is honored as an All-Around State Gymnastics Champion. The team's parents are invited to our school to celebrate their success and to see their sons perform. Allan wishes he had a father sitting there with the other parents, proud to see his winning performance on the parallel bars.

He smiles as he sees me, cheering him on, in the front row.

* * *

1948. The tension between Daddy and his children has transformed the dinner table into a war zone. Mealtimes are agony. There is a shouting match going on between Helen Joy and Daddy. It is close to getting physical. He has ruined her life. Humiliated her with his drinking.

The day after his high school graduation, Allan decides to leave home. He wants to put plenty of space between himself and Daddy. He cannot fix everybody, so he has to save himself.

Allan enlists in the Air Force. Along with a surge of volunteers destined to fight in the Korean War, he is sent to the 3427th Training Squadron at Lowry Air Force Base, Denver. Where he learns to type. He quickly moves from pecking out numbers with one finger to drafting legal documents. Allan's typing skills—his speed and accuracy—make him valuable to the base legal team. He spends his entire tour of duty typing.

Allan receives a letter from Mama. She has filed for a divorce. Daddy has gone. Their lives will be forever separate.

"Separate." Allan mulls over the word.

He, too, will live separately from his father. The sores are too raw to heal. But deep beneath the wounds, Allan feels a glimmer of hope that his Dad will find sobriety and peace...

Allan takes up writing as a career in a roundabout way.

"I figured if I can type," Allan notes, "then I should learn how to write."

And that is why Allan, after four years in the Air Force, lands in the University of Minnesota School of Journalism.

"Looking back," Allan recalls, "I became, in order, a reporter for the Minnesota Daily, a part-time stringer for the

Associated Press, a PR guy for Northrup King, a partner in a small PR firm and, finally, an account executive for Colle McVoy, an advertising firm, where I stayed for 30 years. Moved through the ranks to Chairman and CEO."

Allan is happy in his choice of a career in advertising. The boy who led his sister into a fun-filled world, one of the imagination, ended up making people laugh while doing business.

When your world is turned upside down, a positive attitude, polished with a sense of humor, makes all the difference...

In the quiet of their suburban St Paul home, Allan and his wife, Lois, faced a lifetime of challenges. Early in their marriage, Lois was diagnosed with a neurological disease that weakened her entire body and eventually cost her the use of her arms and legs. Her career as a high school biology teacher had to end. For Lois, life wasn't about her limitations. It was about finding ways to be involved in productive activities. Lois founded a book club, sang in a chorus, baked and cooked wonderful meals. She and Allan were active in church. They raised Arabian show horses as a hobby. They were frequently found at the theater or a museum.

Laughter was no stranger in the Hietala home.

A baby girl needed a mother and a father. Gwynn was an infant when she came to join the family. She grew to be a beautiful woman, a health analyst, and a loving helpmate to her mother. With her daughter at her side, Lois's world widened.

Lois was on fire as a leader and activist for the disabled. Countless churches in Minnesota know her name. They became disability accessible under her watch.

* * *

It is the night of Gwynn's wedding. The bride and groom perform the wedding dance. Now, the guests are dancing. Lois is carried away by the festivities. Handicapped or not, Lois wants to dance. She throws all caution to the winds, invites her brother-in-law, Oscar, who has suffered a stroke, to escort her to the dance floor. For a brief moment, they are flying, like Fred Astaire and Ginger Rogers. Then, suddenly, their feet won't move. They seem to be glued to the floor. They look at one another. Puzzled. Their eyes travel down to the offending feet. Lois's right foot and Oscar's left. They discover that Oscar's left size 13 shoe has landed squarely on top of Lois's right foot. Neither has feeling in those feet.

A good Samaritan unsticks them. Leads them, laughing, off the dance floor.

"It was a great dance," Lois says. "While it lasted."

"Amen!" says Oscar.

* * *

Gwynn gave Lois and Allan a granddaughter, Zoë, whose dark curls encircled a head filled with a curious mind and a zest for life. Gwynn and Zoë were a constant in the care of Lois.

There was nothing more heart-warming than to see Lois holding Zoë in her arms.

To feel her joy at living to see her granddaughter about to enter her teens.

When Lois passed away several years ago, their home became strangely silent. Allan sorely missed the effusive energy that Lois radiated as she tackled an always growing list of projects. The sound of her voice, eager, as she planned her participation as a leader in community events. Dinner parties with close friends. The sweet smell of almond cookies baking in the oven. The busyness of a life fully lived.

Allan has dipped into the well of Lois's remarkable energy. He has found happiness in continuing her legacy. He lives alone with his dog, Cooper, to warm his feet on a cold night. Allan is alone, but he has no time to be lonely.

Allan's alarm goes off every school day at 6 a.m. At seven, he is out the door and on the way to pick up and deliver Zoë to school. Then, to return at the end of the day to bring her home. Allan assists Gwynn, a single mother, in the raising of Zoë. At ninety, he continues to act as a second father to Zoë. He is proud of Zoë, who is soon to be off to college, a serious student and a track star.

Allan is strongly committed to helping at-risk teens through his longtime work in non-profit organizations. Local firms frequently seek his counsel on business matters. He reaches out to friends, most of them widowed, plans weekly lunch dates and participates in several book clubs.

Today, as I often do, I reach for the phone to call Allan. His bright spirit never fails to uplift me. Life is a serious business. He also suffered the pain and anxiety that was mine as we watched our father descend into the dark world of alcoholism.

"Allan," I say, "you took my hand and we escaped into a better, kinder world. You gave me a precious gift—the gift of finding and cherishing humor in the ridiculous. The bad times. The everyday. To laugh at myself. And sometimes to laugh at others."

"Thank you," I tell him, "for being my brother."

6.
DON'T FORGET
TO STOP THE PAPER!

ONE FINE SPRING day when I was four going on five, Helen Joy took my hand and led me to the brown Gothic beauty of the Sumner library in Minneapolis. She left me on my own in the children's corner. I hadn't quite learned to read, but decided to look at a book to take home.

What I remember next is as clear as if it happened yesterday.

Helen Joy and I were returning home. Mama was in the kitchen sitting by the stove. She was baking doughnuts in a pot of hot oil. Her face was red, sweat pouring down her forehead. I ran to her side, shouting the news, "Mama, I can read! Listen!"

She shut off the stove, moved the chair to a safe distance away from that dangerous hot oil. I snuggled into her aproned lap, breathed in the sweet smell of doughnuts and read to her my first book, *Jo Boy.*

Mama was proud of me, and so was I.

All four of us called Mama "The General." Mama ruled the roost, awakening us early in the morning with her high soprano, "Rise and Shine!"

Her voice lifting gloriously to a high C, as she did almost

every school day morning during our childhood. We tried to hush her when we were teenagers, but with Mama being both Mama and The General we lost the battle. We never had an alarm clock, we had Mama. Miss Sunshine. Thanks to her, we are all early risers. Thanks to her, I have always forgone the use of alarm clocks.

Perhaps deep down I still yearn for Mama's beautiful morning song.

Mama approached her children in the most gentle way. She never raised her voice in anger. Instead, she suggested that we "might like to do" whatever needed doing. We all thought that was a grand idea.

I was the third child, lost in the middle between my two older siblings, Helen Joy and Allan, and younger brother Gene. I was a tag-along child. Like a dog, I followed Mama wherever she went. To the basement to wash clothes, the yard to hang them on the clothesline. To the garden. To make the beds, to dust, to clean. To iron. To wallpaper. To shop at the market and the drugstore. Where Mama went, I went.

And all the while, she listened to me. Talked to me.

Mama had been a school teacher. She studied at the university in Grand Forks, North Dakota. She loved teaching little children. Although she gave up her career in order to raise us, she didn't stop teaching. We were her students, fortunate to have her attention.

Mama taught me a world of things. Our walks were frequent and special. They were filled with lessons.

I remember walking past a little girl who wore a dress I had outgrown and given to her family.

"She didn't even say thank you," I pouted.

Mama gave me a quiet talk about graciousness: "You don't do nice things in order to be thanked."

When I am tempted to say something nasty, I remember Mama's caution: "If you can't say something nice, don't say anything at all."

Early on, she taught me about equality when she allowed me to pick my own friends, regardless of ethnic background. This was in a time when other parents disapproved of my choices. It was years later that Edna Mae, my best friend, and I, realized that she was brown and I was white.

Mama was a sounding board for my ideas. I still can picture her late at night in the basement, washing clothes, ironing, listening to my school essays, speeches, clarinet and vocal solos. Believing in me. Encouraging me to do my best.

Sometimes you overhear someone talking about you, saying things that hurt. Things you don't want to hear. Or things maybe you were meant to hear.

Maybe getting hurt can be a good thing?

The auditions for the part of Captain Kidd, the mean pirate, were taking place at the school. This was the leading role in the operetta to be presented to the community. I had never performed in a play, but we were a family of singers and dancers. So, I studied the songs that Captain Kidd was to sing and I went to the school auditorium to audition. I sang in my clearest, sweetest voice. The teacher thanked me; said I didn't quite fit the role and excused me.

Then, as I was leaving, I heard her say, "Such a pity. Lila is so shy. If only she could sing out like her big sister."

Hurt, anger, and tears. Mama wiped them away and suggested I think about who Captain Kidd is, how he sounds and moves. I needed to become him on that stage. And I mustn't be shy.

Into the back yard I stomped to vent those bad feelings. I felt mean. Meaner than I had ever been. Mean as that old Captain Kidd. I would show those teachers, everybody, that I was not shy.

I was Captain Kidd, on board that pirate ship. Angry. Cruel. Staggering about and stomping as I walked on that imaginary deck, shouting:

Oh I'm the terrible Captain Kidd,
Upon the seas I roam.
I throw my victims overboard
And make them swim back home!

Repeating that song over and over and over, louder and louder and louder, until I got all of that shyness out of me!

Mama and a crowd of neighbors rushed over to see the source of all that noise. They congregated around our back yard to cheer me on. Later, they would celebrate the news that shy little Lila got the lead in the community operetta.

The polio epidemic of the '40s and '50s raged through the country. There was no cure. No vaccine. Sister Elizabeth Kenny hired Mama to greet visitors as the receptionist at the Kenny Institute for polio patients. Mama's powerful voice echoed throughout the halls.

Mama arranged for me to interview Sister Kenny as part of my ninth grade career project. Sister Kenny was famous. I had never been in the presence of greatness. My heart raced as Mama brought me to Sister Kenny's office. Sister Kenny sat behind her desk, her halo of white hair shimmering in the light. I trembled when Mama introduced me.

"Sister, this is my daughter, Lila Lou." Sister smiled warmly as she paused and said, "Lila, you have a beautiful name."

From that day forward I loved my name. The sound of it has brought a feeling of being known and loved.

Sister Kenny developed a treatment involving hot compresses for polio patients that was frowned upon in her native Australia. Despite being rejected by the medical community, she remained determined to pursue what she thought was right. She left Australia to meet with the Mayo Clinic, which helped her found a hospital in Minneapolis. There, her innovative treatment gave comfort and hope to polio patients from all over the world.

The wards overflowed with patients of all ages. Though there were many successes, Mama saw up close the tragedy of lives lost to the disease. And lives changed forever due to paralysis of legs, arms, necks, and–in extreme cases–the entire body. Mama cried over the death of a sweet little boy of five.

Some lost the ability to breathe and were placed in pressurized iron lungs. One such case was an inspiring young woman named Pearl Mueller. Pearl's entire body—except for her head and neck—was encapsulated in an iron lung, never to escape. Pearl was an artist. She had dreams to fulfill, no matter the obstacles. Dreams of creating something beautiful while trapped in that unbending prison of steel. Pearl asked Mama for paper, paints and brushes. A makeshift easel that could be placed beside her head. An assistant to place the brush between her lips. Pearl was in business.

Years later, after she retired, Mama facilitated an art show in celebration of Pearl's astounding courage and that of other paralyzed artists. She brought it to our nation's capital.

Looking back, I see that Mama had that same kind of courage. Mama's blood was rich with the strong prairie spirit of her Finnish immigrant parents. Hardship, death and loss were no strangers to the families who left poverty and drought in Finland to find a better life on the farms in rural North Dakota. Only to find that bad luck had come along with them.

Mama bore this bad luck, too.

While still very young, Mama lost a newly-born sister, Martha. At fifteen, she lost her precious younger brother, Arnold, who died of diphtheria after returning from a church picnic. Then came the Drought. And later, the loss of the family farm during the depression. Finally, the death of her father.

"When Arnold died," Mama told me, "it was as if I had lost my own son. I was the one who took care of him. He was the light of my life. This was the only time in my life that I crumbled, that I wasn't strong enough to go on. Your grandmother sent me to stay with a family friend, Edie, who prayed with me and gave me an understanding that God was listening to my grief and would carry me through."

Then came the heartbreak of parting with my father. He was a talented musician—could play most any instrument. I remember him playing *Chopsticks* on our piano with his elbows, his small lean frame and jet black hair, always dressed to the nines in a crisp white shirt and a dark suit. I remember him teaching me to play the clarinet. He had a professional band from the time he was a teenager. They were known all over the Dakotas and Minnesota for their radio show, which began with the popular song *Hold That Tiger.*

Although music and his band had always been his first

love, Daddy had to bring in a steady income in order to provide for his growing family. He was a barber by profession and owned his own barbershop. He was a musician by night. When some of his band members left to join the Lawrence Welk Band on television, Daddy felt cheated out of a great opportunity. He became depressed and angry. He took to drink.

My memory of that time is foggy, but I still get a tight feeling in my stomach when I think of the time when Daddy brought a young lady home.

She was beautiful, in a red dress like a Broadway star. Mama was wearing a house-dress with a floral pattern, the roses faded into obscurity. There was a greasy stain across the front. Mama and we four children sat in a row facing Daddy and the lady. Daddy was telling Mama something that made her very sad. I was too young to understand what he was saying. Daddy and the lady left together. I cried, because I was afraid that Daddy wasn't coming back. Mama tucked us into bed. She was crying, too. She didn't sing to us, as she usually did.

I awoke with the sound of a door slamming. Then I heard Mama sobbing. She was out on the porch in her nightgown, in the middle of a snowstorm. Her bare feet sunk in deep snow. She was freezing. I pulled at her. *Mama, come in!* She seemed to be in a place far away, like in a bad nightmare, one so sad that all she could do was cry. I was so cold. I pulled and pulled at her until she finally woke up and let me lead her back to the warm kitchen.

After that night, for a long time, I fought sleep. I would lay awake for hours. Tense. Listening for Mama crying on the porch. Listening for something or someone to steal into my bedroom with the intention of harming me. This went on well into my twenties.

Many years later, I learned that on that terrible evening Daddy told Mama he intended to leave us to live with the lady. But that never happened. Maybe it was because she had met four little children who needed their father.

As the years went by, Daddy was largely absent from our family doings. He loved us children, but he was not involved in our lives. He was a mysterious figure who went off every morning before breakfast to work in his barbershop. He sat in silence at dinner, then disappeared until well after our bedtime.

The singing-dancing Hietala family stopped singing and dancing. No more Saturday night entertainments. Our father was not around to join us. He was off with the remnants of his band. I could smell the drink when he came in the door.

There was a toxic atmosphere at the dinner table, the air filled with an argument about to erupt. Helen Joy, the eldest, then a teenager, was seething-mad at Daddy. When she spoke out against him, things turned violent. Their voices raised to the point of shouting. The rest of us—Allan, Gene and I—ate our food in silence. Mama tried to keep the peace, but her voice was lost in the terrible noise.

My high school debating partner, Eleta Sanderson, would often invite me for an overnight at her house where we would work on our presentations for upcoming debates. (I must interject that those sessions really paid off. Eleta and I, as sophomores, beat the arrogance out of two North High seniors, and came back to Henry High with the Regional trophy.)

I loved to go to Eleta's. She was an only child; her house was quiet. My anxiety was replaced by a soothing calm. Love, not tension, floated in the air at Eleta's house. Her parents were happy. I wished I could live there.

Eleta's parents invited me to spend a vacation week at their lake cabin—our family never took vacations. That week at the Sanderson cabin was transforming. Eleta and I took long hikes in the woods, sat by the lake, content to do nothing but breathe in the fresh air, the scent of the tall pines framing the water. Back in the cabin, Eleta's mom and dad fried a trout for dinner and we all laughed at the story of how he fought to snag that fish. I wanted to keep that peaceful feeling, the laughter, carry it inside my suitcase on the way home.

It was early evening when the Sandersons stopped in front of my house to drop me off. Mr Sanderson got out of the car to unload my suitcase. As we stood there beside the car, Daddy staggered over, as drunk as I'd ever seen. Lurching and sobbing, "Lila, my little girl…"

The humiliation was too much to bear. I tore into the house and up to my room. Mama told me she had asked father for a divorce.

This was the last time I was ashamed of my father. He left the next day. And I was relieved. But the pain and shame he had caused me, Mama, my brothers and sister, was to be buried deep inside me for decades to come. I never spoke of him. It was as if he had never existed.

I moved through my senior year in high school, outwardly happy, involved in numerous interest groups–solo clarinet in the band, debate, speech and essay competitions. As president of a Junior Achievement group, I helped produce a weekly Saturday teen show on Minneapolis radio. One night, Miss Hansen phoned me. She was unable to get a substitute teacher for her senior English class. I remember teaching a session on the poetry of Carl Sandburg, amazed that my classmates weren't throwing spitballs at me.

Ultimately, I was named class salutatorian and the recipient of several scholarships. This was the outside of me. Inside, I was an angry, fearful person. Angry at a father who was never there for me. Each day afraid that he would round a corner, return to revive the shame that had come to live inside me.

Even my wedding day was tinged with anxiety. I was consumed with the fear that Daddy would come to make a scene. But Mama told me that he was now sober. I could safely ask him to walk me down the aisle. He arrived in a tuxedo, looking sober and handsome. I took a deep breath and said a prayer of thanks. He was fully there for my wedding.

Daddy was overcoming his demons. He found a new life of sobriety with his sisters and their families in California. He returned to his music and discovered painting as a hobby. Our visits were few, but I was glad to see that he was happy.

Time is a slow but effective teacher. It has brought me forgiveness, understanding, and gratitude for the good days, however rare, when Daddy was a father who made music with his children. The day came when I was able to smile at the remembrance of Daddy sitting at the piano, singing with us kids. Daddy giving me his prized clarinet on my first day with the band in middle school.

Mama struggled after the four of us, now grown, left her alone in the house. It seemed too quiet without us, so she moved to a little cottage and began to spend time with her friends.

* * *

1962. One evening, Mama and a girlfriend got up the courage to go to the Marigold Ballroom to dance. There she met a Swedish widower with a twinkle in his brown eyes, stories to tell and a taste for adventure. Mama hadn't danced in years. They danced. And danced. And Mama fell in love.

In short order, Mama and Herman were married. Life was no longer quiet for Mama. Herman swept Mama out of her plain, restricted city life, her pink-walled house, into the drama of the world outside. Built a vacation cabin in the north woods of Minnesota where they listened to the birds sing. Watched the deer playing near the garden. Cooled themselves in the fresh breezes from the lake. The Boondocks was our family's summer destination for 40 years.

It was all about family for Herman and Mama. Herman became an instant and much-loved father to me and my siblings and Grandpa Herman to the grandchildren.

Herman didn't just speak. He boomed. Laughed often. He was a triple-Bronze Star WWII veteran, an Army Corp of Engineers sergeant, who, with his troop, bullied his way into the Philippines to prepare for the landing of the Marines. A hunter, woodsman and fisherman, Herman was built like a wrestler, small in stature but with muscles of steel. A beekeeper who yelled, swearing in Swedish at the bears who dared come upon him as he tended his hives. Beneath his rough exterior lay a gentle heart, pulsing with a love of beauty as found in the trees, the woods and lakes of Minnesota.

Herman was on a walk in those woods. He stumbled upon a massive birch burl. He wrapped it in a chain, dragged it onto his pickup and into his Minneapolis workshop. Herman, after months of sawing, sanding, and polishing, transformed it into a dining table and six chairs.

Herman had a passion for fine woodwork. He learned the arts of design and furniture building as a young man in his native Sweden. His garage became his studio—the place where he created that dining table and chairs that, he told me, would one day be mine.

* * *

2020. Altadena, California. Today, as I look at the dark swirls on the yellow surface of Herman's table, I recall the shine in his brown eyes when he moved it into my home. I run my hands over the intricate flowers and leaves he had carved upon its legs. The chairs, their seats pillowed in an elegant shimmer of blue fabric that he had stitched together at Mama's sewing machine.

And I feel loved.

* * *

Fall, 1997. Herman was a no-nonsense, no-fuss type. At eighty-six, he began to feel poorly. After much nagging by the family, he went to see his doctor. Shortly after that visit my phone rang. It was Herman. I asked him how he was doing.

"Not good. Will you sing?"

It took a moment for me to understand that Herman was asking me to sing at his funeral.

Three weeks later, our family gathered at home in Minneapolis to sit with Herman as he lay dying. It was late at night. I couldn't leave his side. I needed more time to let him know how much I cared for him. But Herman knew. Two young men, neighbors he schooled in his workshop, came to the bedroom door carrying a small side table–oak, checkered with squares of rosewood. This was Herman's last project. He had rushed to build it, but became too weak to apply the final coat of varnish. The neighbor boys had seen to it and presented it to Herman for his inspection, and to me as a final gift.

Herman knew. He knew the depth of my love for him. He was returning it one last time.

He opened his eyes, smiled and said, "Here goes the last of the Mohicans!" Herman loved that book.

I sang some Swedish lullabies for Herman at his funeral.

* * *

Mama was alone. Herman had been her light. He had such a powerful presence; Mama felt small without him. Day by day, she withdrew from life. To shrink. Her brightness faded. As always, she was careful to hide her suffering from others. She put on a happy face beneath the glow of her snow-white hair. Laughed with her bridge group and with longtime friends. But it soon became clear that her prairie strength was ebbing.

Our unshakable Mama had stood strong, brought her family through years of sometimes overwhelming challenges. She taught us, by example, to choose grace, rather than anger. Understanding, rather than judgment. And most of all, she taught us how to love.

Now it was time for her to rest.

Mama suffered a heart attack. But Mama, The General, at ninety, was still in charge at the moment of her death. As our family encircled her hospital bed, Pastor Hogenson led us in prayer. Mama was slipping away, but she had to attend to one more piece of business. She called Allan to her bedside and whispered one last order.

"Don't forget to stop the paper!"

7.

ANNA LIISA

1940. ANNA LIISA IS getting ready to go to the beauty parlor in the small town of Floodwood, Minnesota. After working on the North Dakota homestead for almost 30 years, she has come to live with her daughter, Anna Kaisa, and her growing family. Anna Liisa looks in the mirror, sees how her life on the prairie has marked her. Wrinkles, deep brown rivers, run across her once fair face. She runs her fingers through her thinning hair, now white as the snow on the hill in Finland, the one she and Matilda flew down, their skis scarcely touching the ground.

But she doesn't want to think about skiing. It brings such pain. It was so long ago, 1900, but the pain is always there, waiting to haunt her at the most unexpected moment. Why, oh, why, she asks God, did He take Matilda, our *Merry Matilda*, only fifteen, in such a terrible way? One minute Matilda is laughing, her long blond hair trailing behind her as she soars through the air on the skis her father made for her. And in the next moment she lies in the snow, her leg turned backward, broken. Anna Liisa tries to save her. The wound does not heal. The doctor has to take her leg, but the infection finally takes her life. Anna Liisa's heart is broken. She has to endure the pain alone. Esko, her husband, has gone to America.

"How much can one bear?" she asks herself. She is alone.

Anna Liisa holds Baby Joseppi in her arms and watches him die. Poor little boy, so thin, so tiny, at seven months. Anna Liisa cannot get the food her children need to thrive. Esko's fields are turned to dust in the drought, the little seedlings withered and dead. The drought is slowly starving her family.

The neighbors come to bury the baby.

Death is everywhere. Hundreds are dying here in Nurmes, Finland, where the Huotaris have their farm.

Anna Liisa's eyes pool with tears when she relives the day that Esko left. Eastern Finland had been under Russian rule for over half a century. Russian soldiers, dressed ominously in the dark green uniforms of the Imperial Russian Infantry were in the neighborhood. They were going door to door, taking all the men, even fathers, to serve in their army. Anna Liisa saw soldiers knocking on their neighbor's door. Esko had to leave. Esko kissed Anna Liisa a hurried goodbye, and with their oldest daughter, Jenny, fled to the sea, to America. His plan was to find land to farm among the Finns in North Dakota. He will send for Anna Liisa and the children as soon as he takes possession of the land. He will make a place for Anna Liisa and the children, where they will grow and live in peace.

* * *

"Don't forget, Mama, we'll be going later on to get your hair done."

Anna Kaisa is always going places. Anna Liisa is in no hurry to go anywhere. At seventy-five, she moves slowly. She needs time to think about this new modern world where most everyone lives in large cities. After nearly a decade of drought, dirt and dust storms, Anna Liisa has left her farm to a young couple for the price of $3,500. Like so many of her neighbors, she has gone to live with relatives in a town. Money and jobs are scarce. Even so, it seems that everyone in America *expects* to find work, acquire so many possessions, a fine house, and a car. Only 40 hours a week on the job! And beauty parlors to wash your hair. Well, she, Anna Liisa, is capable of washing her own hair, thank you.

Anna Liisa feels lost in the midst of such plenty. She knows too much about pain, hunger and loss.

Anna Kaisa's children are young, the two boys, Sanfrid and Matt, are soon off to college, and the girls, Esther and Anne Marie, are in their early teens. They are curious about their Finnish grandmother's life, so different from their own. Anna Liisa settles down on the living room sofa, plumps up a pillow, and tells them a story...

* * *

1901. Anna Liisa and her four surviving children are on a ship headed for New York. It is filled to overflowing with immigrant families. All are leaving Finland and Sweden to escape from the hunger, disease and death that has spread its tentacles over all of Scandinavia.

They have come from one bad place to another.

They have boarded a ship of Death.

As the ship moves across the Atlantic Ocean, its passengers are dying of diphtheria in increasing numbers. The captain has no place to put their bodies, so families must see their loved ones cast down into the sea. Sikki, nine, plays with a little boy. Anna Liisa learns he has caught diphtheria and is dying. Sikki has been in close company with Death. Anna Liisa must save her children. Hold them close.

She prays for strength. The pain of losing Matilda and little Joseppi is raw. It is alive; it moves inside her. It sends sharp knives across her heart.

"How can I save my children when I, myself, am helpless?"

Anna Liisa moans, "Wherever we go, Death follows."

The ship is quarantined. Denied entry at New York. Anna Liisa cries, hides her weary tears. The children jump up and down. They are desperate to get off the ship where death waits to take them. The voyage finally ends at Quebec, where they barely put their feet on the ground before they are herded onto a train. The children are frightened. They have never been on a train. Loud screeches, steel grinding against steel, alarm them. We're going to crash! We need to find a bathroom! No one understands their Finnish. No one helps the poorly-dressed mother and her children.

The machine, its noise never ceases, carries them across Canada, to Duluth, Minnesota and to the arms of Papa and Jenny who are there at the station in Lakota, North Dakota to take them home.

* * *

1905. It is the middle of a cold winter night on the Huotari farm in North Dakota. Six-year-old Heiki wakes up screaming. His long blonde hair is frozen to the thin wall of the tar paper cabin. Anna Liisa rushes to warm her hands in the pot of water on the stove. She gently warms the side of his head, the side that is stuck to the wall. Heiki is freezing. She lifts him up, holding him close to warm him. Then she wakes the children, all eight of them, crowded together on three small beds.

"Up! Up!" she commands, "Run! Run!"

And they run in a little circle around the small room, around and around, to get their circulation going. It is below freezing in the cabin. The stove is fueled by buffalo dung. They need to ration it out so it will last through the long winter.

The older children, Jenny, seventeen, Sikki, thirteen, Anna Kaisa, eleven and Amanda Helen, nine, know they will have to run many times before dawn, otherwise they will freeze. Anna Liisa has her hands full with the three-year-old twins, Matt and Oscar, and with Ida Marie, the baby, who is just a year old. Jenny and Sikki take the twins and Heiki in hand, making sure that they warm their little bodies in the running game. Anna Liisa wraps the baby, holds her close to her chest. Moves her legs and hands until she sees warm roses on her chubby cheeks.

Oh, she misses her Esko. She feels forsaken. How could God call him so suddenly, without warning? Esko was fit on that bright May day when they hooked up the oxen to the wagon, loaded it with the children, the chickens and their household goods and headed south to their new farm. They had worked on the Lakota farm for three years. Esko was ready to move on to a larger homestead.

Several days later, they arrived at the farm. It was located just 29 miles south of Minot. Bohemian and Norwegian neighbors have put in some vegetables in a small garden to help them survive the winter. Esko was eager to begin work on a small house, a well, and a shed for the animals. The work needed to be done before the winter.

But, on this day, it appeared that Esko was too weary to begin.

Anna Liisa remembers every moment of that day. She relives it in the quiet hours of the nights and days that followed...

Esko is standing with his family, his black hair shining in the sun, his green eyes sparkling with joy and hope, as he looks upon this new land. His land.

"This is our land," he declares. "No one can take it away from us. We will work the soil. Plant the wheat, the rye, the oats, and it will be ours."

Esko closes his eyes, pauses, as if in pain. His smile suddenly melts into a frown.

Esko falls to the ground, this precious ground, and dies.

* * *

Death has followed Anna Liisa from the high ski slopes in Nurmes, Finland to the Ship of Death, on the endless water, and now to the 360 acres of land that Esko Huotari and his family have come to farm.

Let us weep for the widow. Weep the tears she dare not weep, except in the long black night while her children sleep. Anna Liisa has to be strong for the sake of her children.

Let us weep for the children, who will forever recall the sight of their father falling, his legs, arms and body turned to rubber. The sight of their mother's eyes, transformed in an instant, from joy to terror.

Kind neighbors hear of the family's dilemma. They come to help the widow build a one-room house out of planks. They cover it with tar paper. A sod roof. The house size is 12 by 15 feet. They build a small shed for the animals.

There is a window and a door facing east for protection from the northwest winds. Anna Liisa knows too well of the 40 to 50 degrees below zero temperatures in the winter. She has felt the killing winds that sweep the prairie, often accompanied by blinding blizzards.

The neighbors come to dig a well. They dig down 30 feet. Unfortunately, so they think, the water is oily. They dig another well, getting clear water,

Food is scarce.

Anna Liisa orders the children to play under the trees at the far end of the farm. They must not see her slaughter Helgeson, the cow. They cry when she tells them what she has done. But they are hungry and the winter is long. The neighbors bring sacks of potatoes. Anna Liisa sees that the potatoes will make hearty soups for the long, cold winter.

In her prayers, as she works on the farm, turning up the soil, Anna Liisa thanks the Lord for blessing her family with good neighbors.

Anna Liisa has no money. Sikki and Jenny leave home to work as housemaids in Minot. Sikki, for a doctor and his family, Jenny for a lawyer. The girls are promised one dollar a week for their labors. The doctor arranges for a farmer to take Jenny and Sikki home once a month so they can give their earnings to their mother.

Anna Liisa's heart aches for Jenny and Sikki. Her girls have grown up too fast. She grieves over the loss of their childhood.

But Sikki and Jenny do not need her pity.

Sikki and Jenny are home for the weekend. They have given their earnings to Anna Liisa. How happy they are to help mama buy food and necessities. They don't need money. They are well-cared for by their employers.

Sikki reports, "The doctor's wife welcomed me like a guest. My English is limited, but she managed to help me understand that it is alright to be sad when I think of my Papa. And when I miss you, Mama. I have never lived in such a grand house. I didn't know how to do my chores. But, Mama, she is so patient, speaking slowly in English so I can understand her."

Jenny tells a similar story. Her English is good. She is learning about the law from her boss, who practices law in Minot.

Anna Liisa is eking out an existence on the farm. She is determined to raise her children. The sun beats down on her, turns her fair skin brown and wrinkled as she works from dawn to dusk in the fields. She borrows a tractor for the heavy work. She soon hires a neighbor boy to work beside her. Then a hired hand. The children grow and help her in the harvest. She sells what she has reaped and is able to keep a cow, a horse and some small farm animals.

A second career as a midwife begins when a neighbor calls her to help his wife, who is having trouble delivering her baby. Anna Liisa is soon called on to assist at births around the area. Her fame as a midwife spreads throughout the southern part of North Dakota.

Anna Liisa has come face to face with Death. She will fight it when a new life makes the journey from the womb to the mother's arms.

Over the years, one by one, her children leave her to

start their own families.

She shares her thoughts with Esko, long dead, but alive always in her heart. Esko, her dearest Esko, who walks beside her, invisible, but who surely hears her. Leads her through the long journey of her life.

"Esko," she says, "We have seen enough of Death. How I wish you were here to know that after you left, all our children lived to become strong men and women."

The story ends.

Anna Liisa sighs, trembles with emotion.

Then, Anna Liisa, my great-grandmother, gets into her daughter's Ford. They head for the beauty shop to get their hair done.

8.

THE RED COAT

Sigrid is Sikki's American name. She carries the pain of a childhood innocence interrupted by sadness and loss. She carries it silently. Those who know her see a woman in her late sixties, a grandmother, a widow, going about a normal life, working as a seamstress, chatting happily with her family and friends. Sigrid does not share her pain. It is too deeply driven into her heart. She does not want to open it. Let the others think she has arrived here in Minneapolis, unscathed, after a pleasant life, like theirs.

She does envy them, these younger, carefree friends. They have no idea what it is like to lose your father, your brother, your sister when you are still a child. And then your little son.

Sigrid remains silent. After a lifetime, she feels her heart sink when she recalls the sight of her father falling to his death. Her mother crooning a lullaby to her baby brother, Joseppi, as he lies in her arms, dying. *Kehtolaulu Ja Hyvaa Yota* (Sleep. Baby, Sleep). Her sister, Matilda, screaming with pain while she endures the horrors of a broken leg, gangrene, amputation and death.

Sigrid remains silent when she sees a boy about the same age as her son, Arnold, when he died. Arnold was eight. He played so happily at the church picnic on that Sunday afternoon in 1924. They brought him home, feverish. The diphtheria that killed so many on the ship that brought Sigrid from Finland to America had found its way to a little boy on a farm in North Dakota.

After all these years, Sigrid's tears are dry. Bottled up inside.

No, Sigrid will remain silent. Keep her secrets. It is easier that way.

"Life was hard."

That is all my grandmother will tell me about her years in Finland and on the farm in North Dakota.

Gram once did share a rare moment of her life in Finland. Her eyes softened as she told me that her childhood home was on a lake. On summer Sundays the whole family, her mother, father and her five brothers and sisters, would walk along the shore to the Lutheran church. In the winter they formed a line, a parade, and skied across the lake to the church. The babies on sleds.

* * *

1945. Gram came to live with her daughter, my mother Anna Marie, and our family. I was twelve, and delighted to have Gram all to myself. Sometimes I would forget that Gram was my grandmother. We were more like friends. I would say we were pals. Gram talked often about the problems of the world. Like hunger, poverty, and sickness and our duties as citizens. We talked about the ways our actions can affect others.

One afternoon she asked me, "Is it ever okay to tell a lie?"

"Never," I said immediately.

"Even if your lie saves someone's life? Saves them from being hurt? There are no *nevers,* no *always* in life."

She and Mama were like night and day. Mama was soft-spoken. Gram spoke out, at 5 feet 2 inches, a one woman crusade for the poor. The workers. The farmers. The unions. For the DFL– the Democratic Farmer Labor Party.

Gram joined a union march demanding better working conditions for garment workers. This led to her arrest and a night in jail. She exploded when she was brought before the judge. Gave him a lecture. Waved her arms and wagged her finger at him.

The mere mention of FDR and Truman would bring her to tears, as would the mention of Mother Teresa to a Catholic.

Our quiet Sunday dinners took on a new life. We kids liked to get Gram going on hot-button issues just to see if that was smoke coming out of her ears. Her blue eyes blazed as she raised her voice, stabbed the air with her fork.

Our eyes rolled. We were not always successful in stifling our giggles.

When we had company, Mama whispered in our ears as we went to the table. "Don't talk politics."

I asked Gram what my grandfather was like. Again, that crisp answer.

"He was strict."

A story that will forever remain untold.

However, I did manage to get some of the story from a cousin.

* * *

1909. Johannes (John) Francis Asunma has his eye on young pretty Sikki (Sigrid) Gustava Huotari. At twenty, he lives and works with his parents on the family homestead south of Minot, North Dakota. Sigrid lives nearby on her mother's farm. She has thick brown hair, is tiny, small-boned, delicate. Her finely constructed face belies the strength of a farmhand. John is handsome, tall and lean, with jet black hair and dark brown eyes.

John towers above Sigrid when he takes her hand and leads her on long walks through the countryside. Sigrid feels safe with John. He is strong, like the father she lost several years ago. Soon they are in love. Their courtship is brief. They recite their vows before Pastor Makala and the congregation. At sixteen, Sigrid is expecting their first child, my mother, Anna Marie.

The Asunmas become homesteaders on land northeast of Minot, near the small town of Pelto. Pelto consists of a few grain elevators, a post office, a general store, a three room school, a bungalow for the three teachers, and a house for the elevator man and the general store manager to share.

Their crops flourish. Wheat, rye and flax. Sigrid is a devoted prairie wife. She milks the cows, cooks for the autumn thrashers. Four more children are added to the family. Helvina, Laila, Arnold and Archibald. The children are the first in the family to complete a high school education. They are bilingual, although Finnish is the primary language in their parents' home.

My mother, the eldest, attends a teachers college in Grand Forks for several years before she returns home to teach kindergarten at the tiny three-room school in Pelto.

* * *

1936. John is ill. He suffers from kidney disease. He is too weak to work. The drought is endless. It is useless to plant crops, because they do not survive in the utter absence of rain. The bank in nearby Lakota closes. Sigrid and John are forced to abandon their farm and move to Minneapolis to be near Mama and her sisters. All are married and living in the same, mainly Finnish, neighborhood.

My home is a short walk from Gram and Grandpa's place. Grandpa is too sick to visit with me. He does not smile as he waves at me from the top of the stairs at their second floor apartment. I don't get to know Grandpa like I know Gram.

When Grandpa died in 1937, Gram's pioneer spirit took over. She was forty-five. Her girls were married. Her youngest, Archie, was in high school, planning to study engineering at a Minneapolis college. Four nieces came to her door one night, in need of help. They were the Kyllonen girls, ages six to eighteen. Their parents had died within several months of each other. Their Dakota farm was bankrupt. They had nowhere else to go. Gram welcomed them into her tiny apartment, got a job as a seamstress. She mothered them for four years until they were ready to support themselves.

Gram was unstoppable. A quick learner. During her job interview at the garment factory she was asked if she had experience in operating an electric power sewing machine. She lied. Said of course she did. She went over to a machine, watched a woman at work for a few minutes and then managed to fool the boss. She worked at that garment factory for 28 years.

Gram's pay was scarcely enough to feed four extra mouths. But Gram refused to ask for help. She was proud.

"I always pay my own freight," she declared.

On the day she came to stay with us, Gram installed her sewing machine in our dining room. It took a place of honor beside the china cabinet, not too far from the stove that warmed our house. When she wasn't knitting warm sweaters, mittens, hats and scarves, Gram could be found in the dining room making dresses, tops, and rarely, coats.

How I loved those cotton dresses, bright patterns, that fit perfectly, unlike the hand-me-downs from my sister, Helen Joy.

But best of all, I treasured the Red Coat.

I was thirteen, maybe fourteen, when Gram brought the fabric home, took my measurements and stitched together the first coat tailored just for me. It was scarlet, bright as the sun setting over the horizon. I ran my hands over the softness, like cashmere. I felt bold, pampered, wearing it, glad to be noticed when I passed into the halls of the school.

The community library was in the park, conveniently located one block from our house. Our family couldn't afford books, but I was well-provided for by Miss Johnson, the librarian. She carefully screened my books to make certain they were "proper" reading for a young teenage girl. No *Lady Chatterley's Lover*, *Moll Flanders*, or *Ulysses* would darken the doors of Miss Johnson's territory. I moved from Laura Ingalls Wilder's prairie books to Mark Twain's *The Adventures of Huckleberry Finn*. Jack London's *The Call of the Wild*. Pearl Buck's *The Good Earth* and Betty Smith's popular novel, *A Tree Grows in Brooklyn*. I read *The House of the Seven Gables* and became a lifelong fan of Nathaniel Hawthorne. I wrote bad poetry. I entered essay contests on subjects such as "What America Means to Me," and I won some first prizes.

By the time I entered ninth grade, I had fallen in love with literature in all its forms. I began to dream of going to college to become an English teacher.

Gram's formal education stopped at the eighth grade. She was obviously highly intelligent. What could she have accomplished if she had been granted a college education, or even a high school diploma?

Gram decided to help me in every way possible. I put the money I earned babysitting and picking beans on farms into a bank account. Gram added $100 on each of my birthdays, a big amount in the 1940s.

* * *

1949. I turn sixteen in June. Gram gets me a summer job as an inspector at the garment factory. My college fund is swelling. Gram and I start out at 6 a.m., bag lunches in hand, for a long day's work. We travel by bus, then a streetcar, to downtown Minneapolis. We enter a tired brick building. Ride up in a rickety wooden cage to a large hall. The floors are wood, worn thin and uneven by the years. There are no windows, except for several, high up near the ceiling.

The hall is filled with rows of women in cotton house dresses, busily sewing heavy winter coats. The noise of the sewing machines is deafening. The air is stifling, thick with fabric dust. There are racks and racks of coats along the walls. This is where I will spend the next nine hours, with a half-hour break for lunch, looking for flaws and sending them back for repairs.

Gram is sewing at her nearby machine, keeping an eye on me. The boss also watches me. I work slowly at first, afraid I will miss some imperfections. Gram sends signals of approval when I gain speed in my work. Gram and I are a team. Our goal: the University!

* * *

Gram carries a big Thermos of dark coffee. She relies on a hot cup of coffee to boost the energy she needs while working for hours in the ear-shattering pitch of over 100 electric sewing machines. Gram believes that a cup of coffee calms the nerves. Makes all things possible. She also believes that a cup of coffee opens the way to a great visit with family and friends. Especially if they speak Finnish.

Gram never owned a car. But she did fine on a tractor. A car wasn't in her budget. She manages quite well on the streetcar and bus. If she needs to go beyond the city limits, she calls on Herman, her son-in-law, to drive her.

Herman takes her for a three-day visit with a nephew and his family. All seems fine until the next afternoon, when Herman's phone rings and Gram whispers:

"Herman! Come get me!"

"They don't drink coffee!"

After retiring, Gram moved into a high-rise in Minneapolis. She often hosted a morning coffee for her neighbors. When you entered her apartment you came face to face with portraits of President Kennedy, Walter Mondale, and Hubert Humphrey. I imagined Gram serving a dose of politics along with the donuts and coffee.

I am on the East Coast, practically a world away, as Gram is breathing her last in a Minneapolis hospital. She stirs, calls my name, "Lila…"

Laura, my daughter, is there, at her side. Laura scrambles to ease her, to let her go in peace.

"Gram, Lila is here. She loves you."

Gram dies peacefully.

Far away, in Boston, I say goodbye to my friend. My pal.

Mama finds an envelope in Gram's apartment. It contains a generous amount of cash and a note:

After my funeral, please invite my neighbors
for a party.
Coffee and cake. On me.
I always pay my own freight.

9.
THREE LITTLE
WORDS

I WAS SEVENTEEN, a senior in high school on a blind date at a church picnic. My friend, Lois, told me I had to come meet this terrific guy. I was not interested. I was busy preparing for next week's debate tournament. But Lois insisted, so there I was, in the park, and a handsome six-feet-two sandy-haired Crew Cut headed our way. Lois introduced us and left. Bang! The sky opened up, drenching us to the bone. The young man rushed me to the safety of an oak tree.

Oh no! My long brown hair had lost its carefully generated curls. Heavy wet strands were pasted on my eyes, nose and mouth. I turned away from him, trying to hide my embarrassment. Searching for a gracious way to flee. I was aware that he was staring at me, my face, in particular. He grinned from ear to ear and tried to cover his lips with his hand.

"You are a mess," he choked out between spasms of laughter.

"I am a mess," I agreed, laughing with him, at myself.

This young man was carrying me out of an awkward moment, as if he had known me for a long time.

Crew Cut was a gentleman.

His name was Oscar. He told me he was a midshipman, a sophomore at the University of Minnesota, with a calling to the sea. That he loved literature and poetry. We talked poetry for a while. I named Robert Frost's *The Road Not Taken* as a favorite; he favored Coleridge's *The Rime of the Ancient Mariner*. I asked him to recite a few verses.

Something marvelous was happening as we sheltered under that oak.

Oscar began to quote Coleridge's description of a ship becalmed near the equator:

> *Day after day, day after day,*
> *We stuck, no breath nor motion;*
> *As idle as a painted ship*
> *Upon a painted ocean.*
> *Water, water, everywhere,*
> *And all the boards did shrink;*
> *Water, water, everywhere,*
> *Nor any drop to drink.*

Never had I been so close to words spoken with such beauty. Each word a jewel. His voice, evenly metered, deep and rich.

My disheveled hair was forgotten. The world stopped. I was falling in love.

With a voice.

We started dating. Oscar told me that his given name was Oscar Emanuel Sanden, III. The Sanden family came from Sweden to Evanston, Illinois in 1902. His Grandfather, Oscar, had an upholstery business.

One day a young man came to the shop. He was a traveler, willing to work for food and a place to stay. Oscar was impressed by his manners. Carl stayed for a few days. He entertained the family with recitations of his poems. Played his guitar and sang. Asked them to tell their stories. Then went on to troubadour his way west. Carl was Carl Sandburg, though at that time he wasn't famous.

Carl Sandburg's poetry made a deep impression on young Oscar II. He later expressed his love of the beauty of God's world and its people in volumes of his own poetry and in his sermons as a pastor of many churches.

Oscar II studied physics at the University of Texas, obtained a masters degree and went on to receive a doctorate at the Austin Presbyterian Theological Seminary. He was ordained a Presbyterian minister.

"I'm going to marry that girl," he said after laying eyes on Carolyn Pederson, a school teacher, following a church service in her hometown of Clifton, Texas.

With Carolyn at his side, he served several churches in Texas, among them one in La Feria. It was there, in that tiny border town, that Oscar Emanuel III, my Oscar, was born. He arrived in the midst of the hurricane of 1932, held fast in the arms of his father when the winds threatened to carry him away. His brother, John Howard, was born in Austin in 1935.

Oscar II then pastored the church of the future President of the United States, Dwight D. Eisenhower—the Alamo Heights Presbyterian Church, in San Antonio. The family moved many times. There were more churches in Baton Rouge and DeRidder, Louisiana, Centreville, Mississippi, and St.Paul, Minnesota.

In the 1940s, he met a young Billy Graham and joined him on the road during Billy's early campaign days. His lifelong friendship with Billy led him to Minneapolis, to the Northwestern College of Liberal Arts, a Christian college founded by Billy. He served as Dean and taught physics.

The family settled in a house in Minneapolis. Oscar III entered the senior class in a large high school. A bit of a misfit, this tall, skinny boy from a small town in the deep South. He said "cain't" while his classmates said "can't." But he learned to speak Northern English fast and graduated at sixteen, number one in his class.

He won an appointment to the US Naval Academy at Annapolis. However, his parents felt that at sixteen he was too young to leave home. So he entered the University of Minnesota in the NROTC program as a midshipman majoring in mathematics.

I began my freshman year at the U in the fall. Oscar was in his junior year. Campus life can be tough when you are a commuter, working jobs on the side to cover the limits of your scholarship. Oscar worked the midnight shift as a broadcast engineer at KUOM, the university radio station. He was well-practiced in digging ditches, having spent a summer working for a road crew. He spent a minus 30 night digging and spreading cow manure over the radio's frozen lines. My jobs were easier. Department store clerk. Mail girl at a hospital.

Passing each other as we raced to classes on campus. Stealing a moment together over a hamburger at the White Castle. My liberal arts and his science and engineering classes were at opposite ends of the campus. We were on two different planets.

There was the midshipman cruise to South America in the summer of his sophomore year. I cried when he left the following summer for the Netherlands, Belgium, France and Portugal. I was confused. I had never been so sad to see someone leave. It was like a part of me was missing. Why couldn't I stop crying?

In between all of this traveling we had time together off campus. On weekends Oscar drove his father's old Chevy, often having to stop to make repairs in order to keep it moving. We would take in a movie, mix with friends. Attend church youth parties. Study. Skate on the pond down the street.

Or take a walk…

The roads are deep in a January snow that shows no sign of stopping. I resign myself to the certainty that our Saturday night date is canceled. No one should be out on a night like this. But here he is, my faithful friend. He starts talking, fast. "I had a bit of trouble getting here," he says. "Slid off the road twice."

His grin is that of a boy about to open a big surprise.

"Now I'm here to take you for a walk!"

Oscar is fascinated by snow. Growing up in the deep South, he never saw more than a sprinkling of snow. Normally serious, tonight he is like a boy in a candy store. The snow stops as we approach the bridge across the Mississippi. Below the bridge the river flows, silent, beneath a quilt of purest white. No one is about. No car tracks, no footprints. A continuum of white. Unblemished. We stand, frozen as statues. Not wanting to tarnish this white world with the sound of our voices.

A quiet moment. Then, Oscar's buoyancy overflows. I often burst into song. Oscar is one to sing quietly, not often, and never alone. He grabs my hand, plants a kiss on my frozen lips and bellows:

> *Oh the weather outside is frightful,*
> *but the fire is so delightful*
> *Since we've no place to go*
> *let it snow, let it snow, let it snow.*

A bolt of lightning travels through my body, from the top of my head to the tips of my toes. I *know.* I am saying this to myself for the first time. I am in love and will be in love forever with this man.

I fell in love with a voice.

Then I fell in love with the beautiful man behind the voice.

* * *

Spring comes. Oscar will graduate, be commissioned as an ensign, and leave for duty on a ship based in San Diego. I have thought about the future, what it will bring to our relationship. Will we be married someday? That someday seems far distant. We have never used the word love in a serious manner. I have kept my feelings secret.

It is about a month before Oscar's graduation. We are both on campus. I am hurrying by Northrop Auditorium on my way to a British Lit class at Folwell Hall. I hear someone calling me. It is Oscar, running toward me. He looks serious. He is breathing hard. He must have run all the way from the engineering building.

"What is it?" I worry.

Oscar says nothing. He puts something in my hand, turns around, and rushes off, back to his class at the other end of the campus. I look at the paper in my hand. It is a 2-inch scrap, ripped out of a notebook. Its jagged edges folded over like a letter. It is addressed in pencil: "To Miss Lila Hietala." I open it and read three little words.

"I Love You."

10.

THE PROPOSAL

I HAD THIS GIRLHOOD dream about a romantic engagement to a handsome prince. The setting is a garden, the lawn a rolling carpet of lush green. Giant red roses in abundance surround the ornate granite bench upon which I gracefully sit. Shimmering in a ball gown of silver satin. An emerald tiara crowning my long, wavy tresses. There, at my golden-slippered feet, kneels my prince. An absolutely gorgeous young man in his crimson tuxedo, velvet trimmed with gold braid and military epaulettes at the shoulders. He looks up at me adoringly. Asks me to marry him, to be his forever. I say yes—like I need to think about it? He places a giant rock on my finger. We kiss. And kiss. And kiss. And we live happily ever after.

Wake up, Lila! Get real! Forget the ornate granite bench, the tiara, shimmering ball gown, kisses and all the rest.

This is what really happened the night I got engaged, February 14, 1954.

Snowing heavily on Valentines Day. My steady boyfriend has been gone for almost a year. A year can be a long time when you are young and in love. Head over heels smitten. In June, Oscar will be leaving his ship to come home on his first leave as an ensign in the United States Navy.

Mama and I are taking a break in the living room. She is

resting her feet after a long day at the hospital. I am gathering my thoughts about what I need to read for tomorrow's classes at the U.

Looking out the bay window into the twilight, I see a bent-over figure struggling against the wind and blowing snow. Who could that be, coming up the path to our front door?

Mama and I are surprised to see that our unexpected guest is Oscar's mother. I open the door. Carolyn shakes off the heavy snow that is covering her coat. Wipes her frosted eyeglasses. Adjusts the black bun at the back of her head. I start to ask just why she has come all the way from the parsonage in St Paul to the far north of Minneapolis in a snowstorm. On the streetcar, then a bus, because she doesn't drive. And why, at this time of night?

But Carolyn, all business as usual, takes charge.

Odd, how she looks at me as she plops down on the sofa, waving at me to sit beside her. Her usually sober brown eyes are twinkling. I have never seen Carolyn smile so widely.

Cosy, side by side. Carolyn brings a tiny white box out of her sensible black purse. Opens it, takes out a diamond ring, holds it up for me to see. I gasp as she says the words I have long dreamed of hearing.

Well, sort of.

"Lila, will you do me the honor of marrying my son?"

Mama's jaw drops.

I am not easily surprised. I most always have to act surprised when the situation calls for it. But Carolyn has put me into a state of shock. I am speechless. Can't squeak out a sound. Carolyn figures the answer is yes.

She places the ring on my finger. Gives me a big hug.

I leap to the phone. Send a telegram to Ensign Oscar Sanden, USS *Henrico* APA 45, somewhere out at sea…

"Yes! When?"

A bit unusual, a wedding proposal from your mother-in-law to be? You may be wondering why my handsome prince sent his mother to act as a stand-in. Why he didn't wait until his upcoming leave to get down on his knees to pop the question, like that prince of my dreams.

Perhaps it was a letter in which I just happened to mention that a young doctor was asking me for a date. I was considering going out with him.

Reading that letter on his ship at 2 a.m., Oscar turned green. Saw a potential problem. Made a quick decision. Acted on it. In the morning, shortly after his ship docked in San Diego, he was the first customer at Joske's jewelry store. Then, on to the post office to mail a diamond engagement ring to his mother with instructions as to its disposal.

Oscar and I were married in a church wedding in June, just two days after he arrived home on leave. His father, a clergyman, performed the ceremony.

There you have it.
His mother proposed.
His dad married us.
The groom showed up.
And we lived happily ever after.

11.

NAVY WIFE

REALITY SETS IN after a honeymoon trip in Oscar's lime green Henry J from Minnesota to the far Southwest. Our destination, a tiny apartment in the Point Loma area of San Diego. Oscar drops me off and leaves to report to the ship. He returns with a Navy etiquette book that all newlyweds are given. I am to read it, pronto. We have to make the traditional call on the commanding officer and his wife. I am instructed to wear my Sunday best—nylons, gloves and a hat. We are to leave our calling cards. Oscar's card reads: *Oscar Emanuel Sanden, Ensign United States Navy.* My card reads: *Mrs. Oscar Emanuel Sanden.*

I am beginning to think it should read *Mrs. Oscar Emanuel Sanden, Navy Wife.*

Navy Wife! When the stationer hands me those cards, I realize that I have just gotten myself a new identity. One that will require certain behaviors, yet unknown to me. I married a man who is married to the Navy. I make a vow to support him in every way possible.

I may be Mrs. Oscar Emanuel Sanden to the Navy, but back home in our apartment I am a young bride, practicing her culinary skills on her groom. Oscar claims to like the only recipe I have mastered: Betty Crocker's Pork Chops Supreme. He pretends to ignore the frequency in which I serve it. Say two or three times a week.

As a hostess, I take good care of our guests, see to all their needs. I stitch a fallen button on the back pocket of a fellow officer's trousers.

The problem is, I anchor it to his underwear.

After six weeks playing house, Oscar goes off to sea. I get on a train headed back to Minneapolis and my final year at the U.

Another year of separation, but made endurable by the realization that every day of practice teaching is getting me closer to beginning my career as an English teacher.

Armed with a diploma and a job at a San Diego middle school, I take a train west to the state of Washington. Oscar's new ship is in training exercises in Bremerton. He meets the train. Both of us are exuberant at finally being together after almost a year of separation. The captain has given Oscar permission to leave the ship overnight. In the morning he returns to the ship. I am alone in the Evergreen Motel.

This is the darkest day I have ever seen. The morning sky is black, obliterated by rain. Unrelenting. Feeling the need for a walk after the long trip on the train, I put on my raincoat and step outside. Sharp pinpoints of rain pierce my face. I am being attacked by a thousand tiny knives. I stay inside for the rest of the day, making plans for dinner for two at a fancy restaurant.

The dinner hour is long past with no sign of Oscar. The rain is vicious.

I wait... And wait...

A gloom is settling over the Evergreen Motel.

Finally, there is a knock at the door. I open it. There stands my uniformed husband, his navy blue trench coat soaking, a virtual river running down his face. He makes no attempt to enter. Just stands there in the darkness. After several starts, he manages to say,

"I have the duty."

"The duty?"

"I have to get back to the ship. Now."

I slam the door in his face.

He leaves. I cry.

The etiquette book hadn't mentioned "The duty." Bless the captain, who understands. He has a wife and six kids. Later that evening Oscar reappears at the door. My apologies are gratefully accepted. Both of us know I have some growing up to do.

This Navy wife business continues to challenge me. I suppose that Oscar and I will leave the Evergreen Motel and head to San Diego. Together, we will find an apartment near the school, where I will begin teaching in the fall. As it turns out, it is I who travel south to San Diego by train and I alone who find the apartment. Oscar comes down with the ship just after the start of the school year.

Even when things aren't going exactly to your plans, there is always something good about to happen. I meet JoAnne, who is also waiting for the ship to bring her husband, Walt, home to join her. Their baby, Kathie, is five weeks old. JoAnne welcomes me to her apartment for the long summer's wait. We learn how to navigate diaper pins without stabbing the baby. How to function while sleep-deprived. And how not to cry when our men phone to tell us that the ship's arrival has been delayed by another two weeks. JoAnne and I are learning about resilience. We form a close and delightful friendship destined to last a lifetime.

I complete a year of teaching with plans to renew my contract. Change of plans. Oscar receives orders to report for duty as an assistant professor at Columbia University in New York, teaching Naval Science and Mathematics to midshipmen. We settle into a faculty apartment on West 118th street, a stone's throw from the campus. I enroll in graduate courses in speech and theatre at Teachers College. I act in several plays, among them Agatha Christie's *The Mousetrap* and Shirley Jackson's *The Lottery.* Oscar obtains a masters in mathematics.

Although I am comfortable in my classes and with the midshipmen, sponsoring dances and outings, I am lacking in experience as a professor's wife. I am young. Mixing with the older faculty scares me.

* * *

It is 1957. The president of Columbia, Dr. Grayson Kirk, and his wife host a faculty reception. President's House is a six-story Gothic brick mansion on Morningside Drive, two blocks south of our apartment. I pass it often on my walks, and am looking forward to seeing the interior. It was here where General Dwight Eisenhower lived while president of Columbia from 1948 to 1953.

Oscar and I chat with Dr. and Mrs. Kirk in the formal reception line. We move into a crowded hall where a waiter, dressed in a black suit and tie, comes forward to ask if he might bring us a drink. I have never had a drink (anything containing alcohol, that is). Oscar is a preacher's kid, so I have always assumed the same for him. I roll my eyes when he asks for two gin and tonics on ice. I stand there, holding that drink, visiting with passers by. I have no intention of breaking my vow to abstain. The drink is getting colder and colder. Heavier and heavier. My fingers are going numb. I need to get rid of it—now. Oscar is deep in conversation with a gray-haired professor, unaware of my panic. I scan the crowd to see if anyone is looking. I edge back slowly to a giant potted palm. Smile at the professor as I give it a big drink.

Our first baby is due to arrive during the midshipman summer cruise to South America. I have to leave my course work. As Oscar sails off with his students, I, eight months along, fly back home to Minneapolis to have our baby. The news of our daughter's birth reaches him by telegram in Valparaiso, Chile.

* * *

July 22, 1957. I am in the maternity ward in a Minneapolis hospital, having delivered my baby, Laura Joy. I share a room with another new mother who has also had a baby girl. I am sad to think that Oscar has not been at my side during the birth of our first child. It will be another five or six weeks before he returns from Chile. Mama is taking care of her grandchildren and cannot leave them. I am alone in the hospital and will be for the rest of my stay.

There is a party going on in my room. My roommate's husband is there, laughing with her, rejoicing over the arrival of their baby. Soon, the room is full of noisy family and friends, gathered around her bed, bearing flowers, waving balloons, admiring the newborn who is brought in by the nurse. I have never felt so alone. My husband should be here. I look at them and I am consumed by envy. Self-pity. I burst into a fit of sobbing, pull the sheet over my head and smother my cries.

My doctor pulls the sheet off my face. He gives me a tissue to wipe away my tears.

"Mrs. Sanden," he says, "You have had a hard time. It was a difficult birth and you need time to heal. I'm keeping you here in the hospital for the next week until you are strong enough to go home and take care of your baby."

The nurse brings my sweet baby, places her in my arms.

"Laura Joy," I whisper. "We are going to be fine."

Am I imagining that my little baby is smiling back at me?

12.
SEA DUTY

IN MARCH 1959 we welcomed our baby son, Sandy, to the world. All too soon, in the spring of 1960, we squeezed our two babies, their baby gear, and a survival kit of household goods into the station wagon and headed for Boston. Oscar had orders to go back to sea after completing his masters in electrical engineering at the Naval Postgraduate School in Monterey.

During the three year period from 1960 to 1963, Oscar served consecutively on two destroyers. First, as the gunnery officer on a new ship, the USS *Charles F. Adams*. Next, as the weapons officer on the USS *Sellers*. We were nomads. The Navy moved us to four different homes from Boston, Massachusetts to Bath, Maine, back to Boston, and to Charleston, South Carolina.

On October 22, 1962, America came to the very edge of destruction.

The phone in our house at the Naval base, Charleston, rang. Oscar's ship, the *Sellers*, was in Florida for training. He was calling from a pay telephone in the harbor.

"Looks like I won't make it home for the party."

How strange he sounded. So serious. We had no party on the calendar.

"What party?"

He ignored my question. Spoke rapidly.

"I love you. Tell the children their daddy loves them," he said.

"I'll phone you tonight, I promise," he told me. He hung up.

Oscar didn't call that evening. Or any other evening for the next two months. Later, I figured he was trying to warn me that something big was about to happen. That he was leaving on a mission with his ship, but couldn't share any sensitive details.

The Cuban Crisis had begun. The Soviet Union had installed missiles in Cuba to launch attacks on United States cities. We faced the real possibility of war with Russia. A nuclear war.

The entire population of our country held its breath. Parents of the young Navy wives plead with their daughters to come home. My mother called. Come what may, I would stay and wait for my husband, wherever he was.

The admiral sent a message to the wives. Given the gravity of the situation, we would not hear from our husbands, nor would we be informed of their whereabouts. He gave us numbers to call for help in an emergency.

Oscar's ship was on patrol far out in the Caribbean. The goal was to block the Russian ships from delivering missiles to Cuba. This was the Cuban Blockade. Soviet ships headed for Cuba passed close by the *Sellers*. So close that an interpreter aboard the *Sellers* carried on a conversation in Russian with the crew of a passing Soviet ship. While they talked, spooks aboard the *Sellers* tried to gain intelligence as to just what was aboard the vessel.

On November 20, the Soviets agreed to withdraw their missiles. Our men started to come home. But not all of them.

The *Sellers* remained on patrol as a precaution. I received word that it may not return until after Christmas. However, good luck was with us. The children and I picked up their daddy at the pier just in time for tree shopping.

Spring came, and with it orders for shore duty. We moved to Annapolis, furnishing our new home with the knowledge that we would be enjoying it for two whole years. Oscar taught mathematics at the Naval Academy. He took the middies on a summer cruise to Chile. He sailed to Bermuda and back with his sailing students at the helm. The children enrolled in the academy school, where I acted as a substitute teacher. At last we lived together as a family. Oscar knew his kids.

On a bright day in November, 1963, President Kennedy, a former Naval officer, stopped by the mall at the Academy to cheer on Navy. It was football season. Navy was winning. Heisman Trophy winner, quarterback Roger Staubach—aka Roger the Dodger—was there, along with his fellow middies. Spirits were high. Oscar and I stood with the faculty and a crowd of midshipmen to greet our president as he emerged from the helicopter. JFK seemed so happy to be celebrating with his favorite team, even in so brief a visit. He spoke a few words, flashed one of his famous smiles, waved goodbye and went off into the air.

Two weeks later he was shot. The world grieved.

President Kennedy did not live to see the United States officially declare war on North Vietnam and the Viet Cong. On August 2, 1964 when the USS *Maddox*, a destroyer, was attacked by North Vietnamese torpedo boats in the Gulf of Tonkin, Oscar's shore duty came to an abrupt end.

He began to prepare for his next assignment: Sea duty.

Vietnam. I began packing for a move to the west coast where Oscar will board a ship headed for the Gulf of Tonkin.

But first we had to deal with a problem.

I was going deaf.

13.

JOURNEY TO THE
WORLD OF SOUND

TWO YOUNG CHILDREN, a husband soon to join the Vietnam war on a Navy destroyer, and I was going deaf. Looking back, I realize that I always had trouble hearing. Especially men's voices. I sought the front row in all my college classes. Over time, I moved closer and closer, uncomfortably in-your-face, in order to carry on a conversation. I lip read.

And now at twenty-nine, I couldn't hear my kids calling me at night.

Fortunately, my husband taught at the Naval Academy, close to the National Naval Hospital at Bethesda, Maryland. During a visit to Otolaryngology, I received a diagnosis of otosclerosis, a disorder causing progressive deafness due to overgrowth of bone in the inner ear.

I learned that as I grew from childhood to womanhood, I was gradually losing my hearing. Over time, deep in my ears, the tiniest bone in my body, the stapes, had been at work sprouting deposits of bone. Ultimately growing rigid and blocking sound from entering my inner ear.

I learned that—as in my case—hearing loss is often first noticed by a difficulty in discerning the lower tones, as in men's voices and whispering.

My university professors weren't mumbling! It was that little unseen bone causing all the trouble.

My pregnancies caused the disease to run wild.

The doctor recommended a procedure that, if successful, would restore my hearing.

An appointment was made for surgery on my right ear. If all went well, my left ear would be scheduled for the operation the following year. The doctors were to perform a stapedectomy: a removal of the stapes bone and the insertion of a Teflon prosthesis. They warned me that this was a new procedure that could lead to permanent deafness. I was to be one of the first patients undergoing this cutting-edge surgery.

Decades have passed, but I remember most every detail of that day and the days that followed...

* * *

March 23, 1964. I am shaky as I am prepped before going into the operating room. But the kind doctor–the Captain who heads the department–is here for me. He understands my fears and assures me that his main goal is my safety. And to get my ears working again. He tells me this in front of a crowd of interested doctors, all curious to witness this innovative surgery.

I am anesthetized. It seems that only a moment has passed by when...

I hear!

"Wake up!"

"Can you hear me?"

And I reply, "Loud and clear. You don't have to shout!"

Doctors dancing a jig in the operating room while tears flow down my cheeks.

I am asleep for a long night in a quiet room. Suddenly, I am jolted awake by a rustling sound in the bed. What's this? A mouse in my bed? I tug at the sheet near my head. It is the sheet rustling when I move it. I had never before heard a sheet *rustle*.

I play with it.

Next, there are loud noises outside my door. Like a noisy group of women and loads of silverware crashing down. It dawns on me that I am hearing nurses stirring coffee at a station in the hall.

Feeling ready to take on the new sounds of the world, I edge out of the bed to walk to the bathroom. Turns out I am not ready. I am abruptly hurtled into a swirling vortex, the walls, the room moving around me, a vertigo in which I lose my bearings, have no sense of up and down, left or right. I feel as helpless as a rag doll tossed about. I want to sink to the safety of the floor, but I don't know how to do it. If I fall, I might dislodge the delicate implant in my head and destroy forever all hopes of regaining my hearing.

I try to scream for a nurse, but can only manage a feeble "Help! Nurse..."

As I collapse, a strong pair of arms holds me up. Saves me. The nurse soothes me as she lifts me into the shelter of my bed.

She pats me and says, "You need a cup of tea."

Ready to go home. Oscar puts me in the car. And then the sounds begin. He pulls out of the hospital lot into the right lane on the Rockville Pike. A howling, high-pitched machine descends upon us. Terrified, I brace myself for a collision. I slide to the floor. Oscar, startled at my behavior, tells me it is just a truck going by.

I have stopped shaking by the time we arrive at Donna's house. Donna had taken care of the children while I was in the hospital. They are napping, so Donna puts the coffee on while the three of us visit in the kitchen. Suddenly, there is another frightening noise, akin to something like a plane hitting the roof, bouncing up and down, up and down. I flinch at the sound. Start to fall to my knees. What is happening? Donna and Oscar stare at me, puzzled. Then their eyes turn to the stove, to the coffee pot, which is perking. A new sound. Perking.

My new world of sound is a world of discovery.

The children at play, their voices clear, carrying all the way across the yard where I sit in wonder, absorbing their playful chatter.

In the evening, I lie in bed listening to the night's noises. The wind rushing in the trees. A car driving by. A door slamming. A neighbor calling his dog to come in for the night.

The birds in chorus, chirping at dawn. Magnificent!

Our pastor comes to call. He is a tenor with a high, soft voice. Wrong! I have heard only the top layer of his voice. Now, below it are layers of rich, low tones. I keep him talking, so I can marvel at the depth of his voice.

I have sung in church choirs since I was ten. I am in for a surprise when I return to choir rehearsal. I hear the voices of the choir, the sopranos, altos, tenors and basses in all their fullness and richness. I feel like going over to kiss each one of them.

I cry to think of the beauty that I have missed but is now mine, a precious gift from my doctors.

To think of the kindness that is given to me in my journey to the world of sound.

To this day, the voice of that nurse comes to me often, unbidden, but oh so welcome.

"You need a cup of tea."

It never fails to bring comfort and the sure knowledge that the world is at its heart a kind, safe place.

I listen to that sweet, sweet voice.

And then I pour a cup of tea.

14.
AND THE HILLS
DANCE

1978. IT IS 1 A.M. in Alexandria, Virginia. Oscar and I are asleep. The telephone rings, jolting us awake. The kids are far away at a university in Texas. Has something happened to Laura or Paul? I put the phone on speaker so that Oscar can hear whatever bad news it has to relay.

Laura (sobbing), "Mom, Dad, I won first prize for my cabin design."

Dad, "Congratulations!"

Mom, "But why are you crying?"

Laura, "Because they are going to BUILD it! And I'm afraid it's going to fall down!"

This is the beginning of our daughter's romance with architecture. Laura takes a home construction course, wins that prize, and falls in love with designing buildings.

* * *

1964. Laura is seven. Her second grade class is given an assignment. They are to look at some trees and draw them. Laura gathers her crayons and sketch pad, goes to the woods to study the trees. There is a strong wind moving through the trees. Bending them.

The next week I visit Laura's classroom. I come upon a display of crude drawings of trees. There is one that stands out from the others. Laura has captured the wind blowing through the trees. The wind, the trees, are alive.

At that moment, I know that Laura has been born an artist.

Born an artist. Born a visionary who sees the world through her own set of lenses. As she moves into her teens, she turns to paints. Her artwork matures at a rapid pace. Art lessons. Frequent family visits to museums. At fourteen, a request by Eunice Kennedy Shriver to show Laura's paintings in her art show. At fifteen, she is selling her floral paintings.

Laura celebrates her sixteenth birthday with a brief time at The Art Students League in New York. There, she paints with her uncle, John Howard Sanden, a portrait painter. A summer job at The National Gallery of Art in Washington, D.C. offers her the opportunity to spend hours studying the works of the masters.

With her college degree in hand, Laura begins to study under the modernist, Ralph Rapson, at the University of Minnesota School of Architecture. This is where she meets Gary Cabo. Both come away with masters degrees and jobs at a large architecture firm in Baltimore. Laura with an engagement ring on her finger.

* * *

1983. This is Laura's first day at her new job. As she

enters the crowded office she is greeted by a male colleague.

"Here comes Baby Cakes," he says.

In the mid-1980s there are some male architects who don't seem to understand that a young blond female architect can be their equal. Laura holds her head high. She soon proves her worth as a professional, as an architect. Baby Cakes melts into the past.

Gary brings Laura up to Natick, a suburb of Boston, to meet his parents. Laura feels nervous, wanting to make a good first impression. Gary's mother, Elena, and father, Joe, greet them at the door of their home on Blueberry Lane. They enter a living room filled with people engaged in heated conversations. The entire Cabo clan is gathered there: Gary's sisters, their husbands, his brother and sister-in-law, two aunts, several cousins, and his grandmother, Maria de la Luz. Maria was raised in Spain. She is tiny, like a young child. Even though Maria is swallowed up by the wing chair in which she sits, she cuts an imposing figure. Her white hair is pulled tightly back in a bun, giving her a stern, forbidding look. Her dark eyes spit fire as she argues with one of the aunts.

The noise stops abruptly while introductions are made. Then, as if on cue, the entire group resumes the fray, everyone talking at once, voices raised. Their arms thrust out, their fingers pointing.

Someone yells, "Reagan!"

Maria de la Luz is small, but her voice isn't. After 50 years in America, she still struggles with English.

"Those Re—poob—licans!" she screams.

Everyone laughs. Laura understands there is nothing personal in the tone of the arguments. Emotions lie at the surface in the Cabo family.

Elena serves an Italian spaghetti dinner, made from an old family recipe brought over from Italy by her mother.

Not to be outdone, Maria de la Luz slips away into her apartment, returning with a Spanish tortilla.

Laura has fallen in love with Gary's noisy Italian/Spanish family.

After their wedding, Laura and Gary take positions in Boston firms.

They raise their boys within a neighborhood in close proximity to Gary's family. Their babies, Jackson and Cameron, grow up with their Aunt Diane and Uncle David as a second set of parents, and their cousins, Christian, Matthew and Charlotte, as best friends.

Gary is a get-down-on-the-floor-with-the-kids kind of dad. The Cabo home is loud with the cheers of Gary and the boys playing board games. Gary coaches the boys' baseball, basketball and soccer teams. The Cabos are avid fans of the New England Patriots, the Red Sox and the Celtics. They are a close family that does things together.

It is no wonder that the boys grow up to be happy, compassionate young men, each striving to make the world a better place. Jackson is a medical doctor. Cameron is a computer engineer/entrepreneur.

Laura remains at Graham Gund Architects for close to 30 years. She becomes the firm's first woman principal. Her designs include college and university buildings—visual arts, performing arts—schools, hotels, resorts, museums, communities, private homes.

* * *

2012. It is night in Washington, D.C. As my plane lowers for a landing at the Ronald Reagan National Airport, I am dazzled by the beauty of the night skyscape. Looking down from my window, I see the Capitol Dome, the Washington Monument, and the Lincoln Memorial rising up above the darkened city, ablaze in the brilliance of golden lights. Then, my eyes catch a new light in the skyline. A tall building of glass and curves, set in this city of short, masonry structures. It rests several blocks north of the Capital. It is Laura's project–The National Association of Realtors headquarters. Commonly called The Blue Sliver.

I visit the building by day. It sits on a small triangular lot, once the site of a gas station. The building tapers from 60 feet on the south to about 10 feet on the north, where a small tower rises, like a blue sliver of glass at the very top. Bowed glass walls reflect the sun and the clouds. The changing conditions of the weather create a spectrum of blue colors, ranging from deep blue to shades of aquamarine and sea green. The Blue Sliver has joined our capital's historic monuments, a graceful tribute to what we now deem modern times.

The building is small, but its glass walls open it to the sky. It becomes an illusion; it floats outward into the sky, absorbing its blueness. It has no boundaries.

Nature plays a large role in Laura's designs, including the Cleveland Botanical Garden. She designed a habitat for exotic gardens that are found in such places as Costa Rica and Madagascar. The gardens, the trees, grow naturally, as in nature, inside walls and astoundingly high ceilings of glass. The glass is shaped in geometric forms, reminiscent of quartz crystal.

The Baobab tree, known to have a lifespan of up to

3,000 years, is located in the Glass House that is home to the Madagascar desert biome. The Baobab is called an "Upside Down Tree," because of its thick knobby branches that crawl outward along the ground. Its trunk is the widest in the world, up to 16 feet in diameter. So large that it can hold up to 120,000 liters of water. The Baobab in the glass house that Laura designed is now touching the sky.

The little girl who went to the woods to draw the trees, saw them as living, moving beings, has now built them a grand house.

Over the years, Laura created a number of hotels, resorts and communities for Disney, so it was no surprise when Disney called with a job offer. Laura decided it was time to try something new. She began work in Glendale, California as head of architecture in Walt Disney Imagineering. Gary joined a noted Los Angeles firm.

Laura now works as a Senior Creative Director focused on Disney Cruise Line. She is happily immersed in a fantasy world. In her job, she lives inside Disney stories, leading teams of architects and designers who work together to bring Disney fairylands come alive aboard the cruise ships now under construction. Laura wears a hard-hat as she boards the ships, checking to see that everything down to the last detail will be perfect.

2022. Laura's first ship, The *Disney Wish*–a castle on the sea–makes its maiden voyage.

Laura shares an emotional moment in a press interview that I watch on YouTube:

"My dad was a career Naval officer. He had a lifelong passion for the sea. He gave me some unforgettable tours of destroyers, top to bottom. Now, here I am, decades after his death, following my father's passion."

With tears in her eyes Laura says, "I think of Dad when I put on a hardhat and climb aboard our Disney ship. I know he would be so pleased. So proud."

Tears in my eyes, too.

Although architecture and design have been the business of her life, Laura's paintings have always been the thread that has held her spirit aloft. After a busy day working, Laura heads up the hill in the backyard of her Studio City home to set up her easel. She looks to the west at the hills and the mountains stretching to the ocean. She stands in silence, as in a cathedral. She sees the hills, the world, in Technicolor. The landscape, the hills, dancing, with coats of bright blues, pinks, yellows, reds, oranges, purples.

She loves David Hockney. She loves Gaugin and Kandinsky. She loves rich colors. In her paintings, she celebrates the way she sees the world: vibrating with beauty.

The Cabos' mid-century home perches on a hillside. Like a large rectangular birthday cake, it glistens, its white stucco icing trimmed with shiny red doors and railings. Today, Laura is on the hill, at her easel, painting. Her love for this home, this family, this life, overflows as she takes her brush in hand. In the emotions of this moment, Laura sees the mountains, pinks and blues, rising in the distance, the hills below alive in a flowing river of lemonade.

* * *

1957. New York. We name her Laura Joy. She stands in

her crib in the morning, joyful, a lopsided grin on her toothless face. She greets us with a "Hi Dere!"

With these first words, our baby reveals a bright spirit, in love with the world. Eager to see what the day will bring.

I am engaged in a conversation with a nanny when my strong, wiry, Laura Joy, at eight months, climbs out of her stroller and starts off on a walk down Morningside Drive.

The nanny clucks.

"Stop that baby! Walking, and not a tooth in her mouth! Tie her down!"

Being an untried first-time mother, I hurry home to check with my well-worn copy of Dr. Spock's, *The Common Sense Book of Baby and Child Care.* Is Laura Joy too young to walk? Then I call her pediatrician, who assures me that this is all nonsense.

Laura Joy is left to her walking and I to chasing her.

* * *

2022. Chasing her. At sixty-four, Laura still leads me on a merry chase. She runs toward a dream that is waiting to happen. I chase after her, knowing she has created something wonderful for me to see.

Laura awakes early each morning, her spirited energy refueled. Ready to find the joy in something that makes...

the world sing...
the trees clap their hands...
and the hills dance.

15.

GRANDPARENTING:
A MANUAL

LAURA IS OUT OF college, married, happily pursuing her career as an architect, and Boom! I am no longer just a Mom, looking with a bit of nostalgia at my daughter's empty bed. Her old school books, high school pendants and photos gathering dust.

Today Laura and my son-in-law, Gary, had a baby boy and my world changed. I am branded with a new title: Grandmother. I am a grandmother. I look in the mirror and let my new persona roll off my lips. I am a Grandmother.

Hey, wait a minute! I am too young to be a grandmother. I have no wrinkles I can't disguise with a little Max Factor. I don't knit; I have 10 thumbs. I don't have a rocking chair, either.

Now, you, my dear reader, may also have come to this milepost all too early. Let me assure you that once you overcome the shock of being cast as over the hill, you may find yourself enjoying the idea of being a grandparent. Being needed to protect and guide a sweet baby through the joys and perils of childhood.

Many years have passed since I first became a grandmother. Today, my grandchildren are grown and gone from home. No longer in need of a grandmother's attention. Based on my past experience, I have found that being a grandmother is a serious business. If you go about it in the wrong way, you will scar your baby grandson or granddaughter for life.

Never fear! May I suggest you follow the golden rules of grandmotherly behavior as outlined in my best-selling book, *Grandparenting: A Manual.*

Rule 1. Don't brag.

Let's say your grand-baby talks at one month. I realize that you are tempted to boast about your tiny genius at the weekly grandmothers club meeting. Believe me, at least two or three of these grandmothers will swear that their grandchild talked at birth. Bragging can get you nowhere with a group of grandmothers. Their grand offspring are always cuter, smarter, sweeter, than yours.

Say, some years later a proud grandmother approaches you and begins to brag about her highly intelligent grandson, who has graduated high school and is headed off to college. To study molecular something or other. Well, I understand how difficult it is to refrain from bragging about your grandchildren. Sometimes you slip—even I do—and begin to rave. But, having sworn to follow the rule of my manual, I seal my lips. I think about the feelings of my friend, how happy she is when she brags about her grandson, who was, poor thing, only #2 in his class.

DO NOT BRAG!
DO NOT BRAG!
DO NOT BRAG!

Say it three times before each meeting. Three times during the meeting if you feel like you are falling into temptation.

Rule 2. Don't interfere.

First time parents are novices. When baby has his first bath, you must surreptitiously lean in to check the temperature of the water in the baby's bathtub. If it seems scalding hot you might gently suggest that the little mother add some cold water. If she thinks the water is just fine, you must refrain from grabbing the baby and running. As it turns out, the new mother will quickly learn from her mistake. She will remove the screaming baby from the scalding water without your interference. You can be sure that she will ask you to interfere many times during the next 20 years.

Rule 3. Get down on the floor.

Yes! Get down on the floor with the baby! It is highly important that you converse with your grandbaby at his or her level. He or she needs to feel your equal. (Although, actually, the little bugger may be a lot smarter than you are.)

Now, I realize that you may find it impossible to get your body into an upright position at the conclusion of your little chat with the baby. Let me suggest that you carry your iPhone at all times. The fire department will gladly come, sirens blasting, your neighbors gathering round, to help you up.

Do not despair when you see your name in the headlines of the local paper.

Rule 4. Keep your car keys handy.
(A True Story)

Grandparents are called upon to act fast during an emergency. When the school nurse calls to inform you that your eight years old grandson, Jackson, has a rock up his nose, you must be ready to move without delay. You speed down the highway, breathing hard, imagining the worst. How big is the rock? How did it get there, stuck up his nose? You scoop him up from the arms of the waiting nurse and rush off to see his pediatrician, Dr. Ow.

Dr. Ow takes his little mirror, looks up Jackson's nose.

Dr. Ow, "You have a rock up your nose. Now tell me, Jackson, how did it get there?

Jackson (voice muffled by the rock up his nose), "I fell on a rock at recess and it went up my nose."

Dr. Ow, "Fascinating. It just slid up your nose, all by itself, right?"

Jackson, "That's right."

Dr. Ow removes the rock. Pats Jackson on the head, whispers, "Don't put any more rocks up your nose."

Grandparents to the rescue! Be ready at all times. You never know when you may be called upon to rescue your grandchild from a dire situation.

Rule 5. Celebrate your grandchild's achievements.

What could be more blissful than the bedtime hour of your grandbaby? You hold the baby close; the sweet smell of Ivory Soap lingers in his freshly-washed hair. Pink roses blossom over his soft cheeks. His eyelids droop, and he is fast asleep before you finish his lullaby song.

As Baby grows from toddler to kindergarten and primary school, the bedtime ritual changes from lullabies to

Goodnight Moon to *Winnie the Pooh.* Your grandbaby is getting ready to read.

Jackson— I think he was around five, maybe six—and I were sitting in the rear seat of the car. His parents in the front. It was a long drive. I took a book from Jackson's bag, intending to read it aloud.

"No, Grandma," he said. Then he announced, proudly, "I can read it!"

Our ears perked up. Last we heard, Jackson had not yet learned to read.

It was a simple book, *The Cat in the Hat* by Dr. Seuss. We had read it numerous times to Jackson.

Jackson opened it and read most of it before we interrupted him, amazed that he had so suddenly learned to read. We applauded him, excited to think that reading came so easily and early to him. We celebrated at Jackson's favorite restaurant, Bertucci's, with pizza and balloons.

The next day, Jackson's teacher sent home a note:

"Jackson has a very fine memory. Today he read *The Cat in the Hat* word for word, without error. Unfortunately, when given a reading test, he failed. He was unable to read anything beyond the title, which I read to him."

A balloon deflates rapidly.

Jackson's childhood tenacity to memorize and consume great amounts of detail was to be an instrumental part of his character in making him the dedicated and successful doctor that he is today.

Rule 6. Draw close to your grandchildren.

You have taken a vow to stay out of their parents' decision-making. But, you can remain close to your grandkids by creating occasions that allow you to spend time together. They are always hungry. Take them out for lunch after school. Shopping for cool athletic wear. To the library or bookstore. A tennis game. A bike ride.

Or, call for help with a problem.

How do you get a red wine stain off a white cashmere sweater? And worse, you borrowed it from a new friend?

How do you get back on cable TV when it stops in the middle of your daily dose of Turner Classic Movies?

The answer: Go on the internet. But how do you get on the internet when it decides to take a long nap? You can't get on the internet to find out how to get back on the internet. You are tearing your hair out. So what do you do?

I call Cam.

My grandson knows I am an idiot when it comes to tech talk. But, listen, we all have our shortcomings. What is a podcast? Do I really need to know? I've gotten along just fine for 90 years without whatever it is.

Do I need to know how to find the Haptic keyboard on my iPhone? I didn't know it was lost. My iPhone has Easter eggs? Where are they? No matter. I have enough on my plate without them.

As for Facebook, best to forget it. I will not voluntarily reveal the road maps on my face to anyone, certainly not a group of friends.

So my grandson discovers I am not perfect. He sees my weaknesses. My stubborn resistance to change. He is patient and kind as he helps me find solutions to my problems. He realizes that I am a human being, just like him.

Perhaps that is why we are such good friends.

Rule 7. Be available.

Dear Reader, I am aware that as a senior citizen, your calendar is always full. Need I remind you that you are a grandparent with duties to fulfill? Sometimes heroic actions are required of you as you tend to the needs of your grandchild.

Let the following story inspire you to perform acts of courage and self-sacrifice in the face of imminent danger.

* * *

2013. I moved from the Boston area to an apartment in Studio City, near the Cabos' new home. Laura, Gary and my older grandson, Jackson, are at work in their new positions in the Los Angeles area. I am about to drive my grandson, Cameron, to his new school. He is beginning his tenth grade year in high school.

This won't be a bad drive, I think. The school is just a few miles away from the Cabo home. For the most part of my life, I have driven the crowded highways of Boston, New York and Washington, D.C. with bravado. I moved quite easily around Los Angeles in the 1980s. Cam and I travel downhill through his quiet neighborhood, stopping at Ventura Boulevard. We need to cross two lanes of eastbound traffic in order to turn west. The traffic is heavy, the cars are moving fast, well beyond the speed limit. I see a safe lull and move across the road, narrowly escaping oncoming cars whose drivers deliberately speed up when we enter the roadway. Horns shatter our eardrums. They are in for the kill!

By some miracle, Cam and I arrive at the entrance to the school unscathed. Cars enter and block the intersection well after the light turns red. I have to hesitate a wee bit when I am about to turn left into the gates. The cars to my rear sit on their horns, apparently angry, expecting me to join them in a deadly game of Risk.

California drivers have made a great impression on me. It takes awhile for me to stop shaking.

For the next three years, I fought the early morning traffic to drive Cam to the school, returning to deliver him home in the late afternoon. Outside the car there was chaos; inside the car there were a grandmother and her grandson who silently prayed for survival.

How close we were! Screaming in unison when a truck whizzed by within inches of our doors. Delighting in the good moments of togetherness while we were stuck in the car for an hour or so during a traffic jam. We talked and talked. We were both living in a new place, without friends. I knew that Cam missed his longtime friends and familiar places, as I did. But Cam was comfortable in his shoes. It was no surprise that he was eager to make new friends; to experience all that a new life in a California school had to offer. Soon Cam found his place on the debate team, the ethics team, soccer and basketball teams. He began painting beautiful portraits. Honing his writing skills. Making friends. Cam had found his niche.

And I, his chauffeur and confidante, was there to see him do it.

Dear grandparents, Clear your schedule. Make yourself

available, ready to face the unknown with courage. Go forth bravely! There are priceless rewards awaiting you.

Rule 8. Listen to your grandkids.

Kids can be annoyingly persistent. They can be relentless in wearing down their parents when they want something they don't need.

When the boys were preteen, Laura and Gary took them to Italy. They stayed at a château in Tuscany with a most lovable dog. The Cabos had never had a dog. Their jobs were too demanding. Jackson and Cameron fell in love with that dog, Fiorella. Back home, they pleaded, begged, cried, argued, gave all the good reasons for getting a dog. Said they were lonely and sad to come home after school to an empty house.

Nothing worked. No one seemed to be listening to them. Weeks went by with no dog on the horizon.

One day I arrived at their home to see a large pencil drawing of a skull and cross-bones on the door, its evil eyes leering out at me.

The message below this apparition sent chills through my body.

"DOG OR DIE!"

My grandkids were getting desperate. It was now clear that they needed a dog.

And no one knew what lengths they would go to in order to get one…

Mango, the cockapoo, arrived shortly after.

Listen to your grandkids. Or else…

Rule 9. Limit your stories of the "Good old days."

Your grandchildren may not want to hear a lengthy dissertation on the Black Plague of the 1300s, the depression of the 1930s or the shortage of sugar and flour during World War II. They may not want to hear much about the diphtheria epidemic of the 1920s. So, do tell it, but mix in some uplifting stories, for there was goodness and laughter in the people who endured the heartbreak and sadness of these eras.

Rule 10. Laugh often!

Laugh at yourself and the foolish mistakes you may have made in the past.

Laugh with your grandchildren at their foolish mistakes.

Rule 11. Make chicken and dumplings.

Afterword.

Cam, at seventeen, needed a reference on his application form to be a summer camp counselor.

"What is your relationship to this individual?"

"Grandmother," I wrote.

Cam printed a copy for me that I promptly filed. It has lain untouched, unread, in my file cabinet for close to a dozen years. Today I discovered the three words Cam had added:

"Grandmother—MY BEST FRIEND."

16.

AN AMERICAN
PAINTER

IT WAS A QUIET Sunday morning in July, 1973. Oscar's brother, John, and his wife, Priscilla, were settling down in their usual spot, the front pew of the Fifth Avenue Presbyterian Church in New York. Baby Pamela, at twelve months, had been delivered to the nursery. All seemed well. The organ swelled with the music of the first hymn, *Come, Thou Almighty King.*

Suddenly, Priscilla grimaced in pain. She rubbed her forehead. Pushed her dark hair away from her eyes, as if to see better. She told John she had a headache. Left him in the pew to go back to the apartment to lie down. Suddenly, Paster Jones came down from the pulpit. He grabbed John by the shoulder and rushed him out of the church. Paster Kirkland addressed the congregation and called for a doctor. Dr. Wan Gno Lim responded. She and John found Priscilla, lying lifeless, her long black hair, shining, as it spilled over the curb and onto the dirt of the street.

Priscilla had suffered a hemorrhagic stroke at age thirty-three.

Oscar and I traveled from our home in Virginia Beach to say goodbye. To take the baby home with us. Her father needed to grieve.

"Someday we'll be together."

These were my last words to Priscilla in a phone call the night before she died.

Oscar and John had always been close. Oscar would often remind John that without his big brother he would not have attained prominence as a portrait painter. When the boys were little, Oscar would roll out some butcher paper on the floor, give his baby brother some crayons, along with a drawing lesson. John studied art at the Minneapolis College of Art and Design. He began his career as an illustrator and the art editor for the Billy Graham Evangelistic Association. He painted 85 portraits for *Reader's Digest* over the next six years. Think Norman Rockwell when you look at John's early paintings.

John was thirty-four. He had lost his young wife. The mother of his baby. However, John's faith was strong. The road going forward was clear. John would trust in God for strength and guidance. He would put all his faith and trust, all his energy into his passion. John would learn to paint portraits like the masters.

John writes of a spontaneous decision in his memoir, *Face to Face with Greatness.*

I went to the Art Students League to enroll in the Robert Brackman evening class. The great portrait painter was then the most famous teacher of painting in America…The annual League instructors' exhibition was open that evening in the second floor gallery. Each instructor showed one painting. On the opposite wall as I entered was a monumental painting of a young boy… I made directly for it. Hanging beside it was a small painting by another instructor—and it was the most beautiful thing I had ever seen. The painting was of a lovely older lady in a black dress and hat. Her gloved right hand held a white rose. The colors and tones seemed to float and shift with a palpable aliveness. The brush strokes were bold, flowing, and dramatic. The edges of the forms shimmered and melted, one into another. I had never seen such sheer loveliness in all my life. Bending close to catch the signature, I saw for the first time the flowing script that read one word: Oppenheim.

Thoughts raced through my mind: could I learn to paint like that? Was it in fact painted, or did that image just somehow exist in a romantic, mysterious world of its own? Yes, it was oil paint all right—and it was a miracle. I dashed downstairs, my heart pounding, and signed for the Oppenheim class!

In a transforming instant, I made one of the pivotal decisions of my life. Brackman was a great artist as well as a great teacher. But I sensed suddenly that in the Brackman class, my already tightened careful style would only get tighter and more careful. In contrast to the classic solidity of the Brackman approach, the Oppenheim style seemed to offer exciting qualities heretofore foreign to me. To go with Oppenheim would be a 180-degree about-face for me—an adventure into new and unknown realms.

In the Oppenheim class, my excitement was realized. Immediately I left behind the old painful precision in favor of a heart-lifting freedom and casualness. My edges became soft, the brush strokes flowing. 50 tiny strokes were replaced by three broad, sweeping ones. It was a whole new way of working. I was excited beyond words. For reasons that I could not fully comprehend at the time, doors were being thrown wide open for me...

* * *

In 1970, John painted U.S. Senator Peter Dominick of Colorado—his first commissioned portrait. A parade of distinguished American leaders in government, business, education, philanthropy, religion and the arts followed.

He painted official portraits of governors, senators, the presidents' cabinets, church officials, university presidents, philanthropists, famous Hollywood actors, foreign royalty, prominent educators, and corporate heads. Hundreds of portraits. His portraits of senators hang in the Capitol. Federal department heads in their buildings. Governors, in state houses. His portraits of educators can be seen at colleges and universities all over the country.

Many of these marvelous individuals sat for their portraits in John's studio—Studio 1010—at Carnegie Hall in New York. Among them, the Reverend Billy Graham, the great financiers David Rockefeller, Kenneth Langone, Maurice Greenberg and the heads of the six largest banks in America: J.P. Morgan Chase, Citigroup, Bank of America, Wells Fargo, Wachovia, and Chase Manhattan.

John's portraits of violinist Issac Stern and philanthropist Sanford Weill hang in the lobby of the Carnegie concert hall.

His beloved New York recognized him. Among his many awards: the 2005 Portraits, Inc. Lifetime Achievement Award; The John Singer Sargent Medal for Lifetime Achievement from The American Society of Portrait Painters.

John's official White House portraits of former President George W. Bush and former First Lady Laura Bush now hang in the White House.

John's accomplishments were the result of a remarkable talent and energy. But behind the scenes there always was Elizabeth. When John married Elizabeth, we welcomed a talented artist into the family. Beth became Pamela's mother. Our nephew, Jonathan, completed their family.

Elizabeth put her career as a portrait painter aside to raise the children and to work with John. For over 50 years, Elizabeth faithfully insulated John from all the details and worries of his extraordinary life. Freed him to be what he was created to be.

A painter.

* * *

2017. John's 50 years of portrait painting was celebrated with a retrospective exhibition at the Salmagundi Club in New York. There was a sentimental moment when Clay Barr and her daughter, Elena, of Norfolk, Virginia, stood beneath their portrait, painted 44 years earlier. This portrait is one of John's first commissions.

A moment of sadness. Priscilla did not live to see it completed.

* * *

2022. John was in his mid-eighties. You could find him in his Ridgefield, Connecticut studio, brush in hand, bringing life to a blank canvas. Although his health was failing, he finished a remarkable undertaking, an 80-some-feet-long mural, *The Empty Tomb*. It hangs in the Billy Graham Museum in North Carolina.

John would never willingly retire. His hand and heart were glued to the canvas.

* * *

December 24, 2022. On Christmas Eve, just days after completing what was to be his last commissioned portrait, John Howard Sanden, an American portrait painter, laid down his brush and died.

17.

ROBOT WITH
A HEART

SANDY WENT TO HIS father's tool shed in San Diego to find some empty cardboard boxes. He liked to go in there with his father. He liked to watch Dad, who was always fixing things that were broken or making new things that worked better. But now, his dad was away on a destroyer fighting the Vietnam War. Halloween was around the corner. Sandy, at seven, was on his own. He needed to come up with a costume all by himself. Sandy came across a battery, some wires, and a tiny propeller. His mind was whirling. With a cardboard box for the body and a cardboard box for the head, he was going to make a robot. Now, to figure out how to do it.

What would Dad do? Or, what would Leonardo do?

More than 400 years ago, Leonardo da Vinci designed a knight known as "Leonardo's Robot."

In the 1960s a little boy called Sandy, on his own, reinvented the robot.

Fast forward to Halloween. Sandy wins first prize in the second grade costume parade. I, his mother, his big sister Laura, Cousin Flora, Markie (the Irish setter) and Sandy the Robot are trick-or-treating in the neighborhood. Moms, dads and kids cheer at the sight of the robot with a whirling propeller on top of his cardboard head. But then something happens. The propeller stops spinning! Our little inventor tries to fix it, to no avail. So he does what any other frustrated inventor would do. He drops down on the sidewalk, kicking and screaming, and cries his heart out.

Markie licks his face.

Sandy is late coming home from school. He is supposed to walk with his big sister, but she lost track of him while stopping to talk with her girlfriends. I am getting worried. Just as I am about to head up the hill to look for him, he comes into the kitchen, shirt torn, face, hands, jeans and shoes covered in mud. A sheepish smile on his face. He has been in a fight. Not allowed. I demand an explanation.

"Bobby said that his mom is prettier than you! So I pushed him hard into the mud. And he pushed me back. And then we laughed."

I try to hide a smile. I give him a cookie.

Four years of the Vietnam war go by, with Dad far away on ships at sea for the most part of these years. Sandy takes over Dad's role as Mr. Fixit. Some might say that Sandy is a bit too young to be Mama's Mr. Fixit. But whatever gifts I have, problem-solving broken gadgets and machines is not one of them.

One dark night I am driving the Plymouth home, the kids in tow after a visit to Weiner Schnitzel. I am moving merrily along at 50 miles per hour through heavy traffic when the accelerator pedal goes limp. Not good. The car slows abruptly, then stops. Cars begin honking in an angry chorus. I freeze, not knowing what to do. Sandy springs into action, dives down to the floor, figures that the pedal has slipped off its spring. He fixes it. Sandy stays on the job, repeatedly reconnecting the pedal as it slips off, keeping us safe for the rest of the way home.

* * *

In 1967 the ship comes home from Vietnam for Christmas. Dad has missed the past two. So, we are excited to take him along to the tree lot. Sandy rushes over to a tall evergreen.

"Too tall," Dad says.

We brought it home anyway. The kids place it beneath our living room chandelier.

"Not there. The chandelier is in the way," says Dad.

"No, Dad. We always put it there."

Sandy, now nine years old, goes to the garage, returns with a ladder, climbs up to swing the chandelier aboard a hook he had installed in the ceiling. Problem solved.

Dad realizes what he has sacrificed over the years.

When he was a preschooler Sandy wrote words and numbers backwards. By the time he reached third grade it became obvious that Sandy had a problem. Although he was trying hard, Sandy had made little progress in reading and math skills. I knew that kids learn to read at different ages. But Sandy and I had come up against a wall. Sandy was struggling. He had fallen behind his classmates and I was at a loss.

The Saturday Review of Literature published a story that gave our family a new direction. The cover featured a photo of a young boy, the son of an engineer. The caption read: "DYSLEXIA." This was a new word to me, and, at the time, to most of the general public. I read on. Although highly intelligent, the boy in the article had been diagnosed with dyslexia, a condition in which there is a difficulty in learning to read or interpret letters and symbols. A common symptom of dyslexia: reversing sequences of letters and numbers. I thought, *This is Sandy!*

I immediately sought professional help. Sandy began a private program of tutoring with an experienced teacher who confirmed my diagnosis. On his recommendation Sandy enrolled in a school dedicated to dyslexia remediation. He spent his days in a class of 12 boys, all suffering from dyslexia. On the first day, his teacher gave each boy a white rabbit. Mr. Bun Buns became a symbol to our family that Sandy was on the way to overcoming this mysterious thing called Dyslexia.

This was to be a long, slow journey. Years of pain and discouragement, as Sandy moved from tutor to tutor. Often he was not able to see the progress that we saw.

It is almost impossible to convince a child that he is bright when he sees that his peers are ahead of him. When he judges himself by this one problem. Thinks he is stupid, although tests reveal him to be highly intelligent. We could only tell him that we believed in him. That with patience and hard work he would catch up to his classmates.

I wish now that I had known that Albert Einstein, the most influential physicist of the 20th century, did not learn to read until he was nine years old. Einstein was dyslexic, along with Winston Churchill, Carl Jung, Thomas Edison, Bill Gates, and Steve Jobs. And 10 percent of the population in the USA.

And Leonardo da Vinci, who liked to sketch and make notes of ideas for his inventions. These notes were written backwards from right to left, in a mirror image.

Despite his misgivings, Sandy was fierce in his

determination to overcome. And he did. He enjoyed academic success in high school and during his college years. Life got better.

* * *

1970. Lake Little Too Much. In Minnesota, just north of Lake Big Too Much. Indian territory in the past. Vacation cabins now ring the lake. Big Red, a retired World War II vet, his face hidden behind a thick rusty beard, comes by to visit Grandpa at his cabin. At some point, he invites Herman's grandson, Sandy, to take a spin around the lake in his battered old seaplane. Up they go, around and around, finally coming down on the lake to execute a beautiful parking job at the dock.

Sandy, eleven, knew then that he would one day fly. Leonardo, a man who never actually experienced flight, well understood how seductive and life-changing it would be:

> *When once you have tasted flight, you will forever walk the earth with your eyes turned skyward, for there you have been, and there you will always long to return.*

Sandy's eyes were forever turned skyward.

* * *

1973. The house is filled with the noise of two babies and two teenagers. Our Erik is nineteen months when his baby cousin Pamela, at eleven months, comes to live with us.

Her mother, Priscilla, has died suddenly at thirty-three. Sandy, fourteen, and Laura, sixteen, are lost in the sadness, the cries, chatter and demands of the two little ones. Cousin Helen, eighteen, is here from Texas to help care for the babies. Our house is bursting at the seams. Bodies and babies everywhere.

A father sees that his son needs a quiet place to be alone with his thoughts. He asks Sandy to help him build a tree-house. After years at sea, Oscar is happy to spend time with his son in a giant Mr. Fixit adventure. The two work as one from beginning to end, carefully drawing up architectural and engineering plans, selecting materials. Constructing. Teaming together to the very last nail.

Laura Joy joins the team, reaffirming her desire to study art, perhaps architecture, in college.

Sandy's Place. High up in a tall oak in a mid-century wonder, a boy can look up into the sky and dream his dreams. Relive the time he and his dad created something marvelous.

* * *

September 25, 1981. Captain Oscar Sanden, USN, conducted his last official act in the Navy: the commissioning of his son, Conrad Paul "Sandy" Sanden, Ensign, USN. Paul was assigned to a Patrol Squadron in Brunswick, Maine as a flight officer, P-3C airplanes. He served for seven years, then left the Navy to fly for Delta Airlines. He retired as a senior captain in 2020.

Paul had fulfilled the dream that first consumed him when he was little Sandy, circling above Lake Little Too Much.

* * *

2019. Carmen and Paul invite 40 friends and family to travel with them on sleighs to the top of a Park City, Utah mountain to celebrate their sixtieth birthdays. The dress code is your warmest winter outfit. Ski clothes. We board the sleighs in the darkness of a cold March evening, the wind raw and the temperature well below zero. Furry blankets are provided. We huddle beneath them. As our sleighs rise up the steep mountain, we are enchanted by the lights of the city below. Park City has become a winter fairyland, its lights twinkling, flashing in and out through the blurred lens of heavy snow. Up, up we go, climbing almost vertically to reach the very top of the mountain and the warmth of a yurt transformed into an elegant Norwegian restaurant. A large black Norwegian *Jotyl* stove and warm cups of *glogg* take the chill off our bones. We dine on a five-star Scandinavian meal.

Champagne and birthday cake are served as we sing the Happy Birthday song and toast the couple.

The party seems to be ending when Mark, a close friend, rises to his feet.

This is not the end of the party!

We're gonna have ourselves a WEDDING!

This is a surprise wedding. Paul comes forward to stand beside Mark, who is to perform the ceremony. Carmen's mother, Doris, and I are in place to act as ring bearers. This is a first: ring bearers at eighty-five! We are among the handful of folks who are in on the surprise.

But where is Carmen? She is nowhere to be seen. All eyes go to the door. Big silence… Longer silence…

Someone yells, "Runaway bride!"

That did it. There is Carmen, very much there, an angel in white silk, floating down a path to wed my handsome son.

Carmen is an event manager. She outdid herself with this one.

Carmen regards good health as a miracle after a battle with cancer some years ago. Carmen and Paul approach each day as a gift, to be opened, enjoyed, and shared. Their day begins with a specially-brewed cup of coffee and a long hike with Shylo, their golden retriever. They move together through time, celebrating nature as they hike, ski, bike through the states and Europe.

Paul is happy to be her Mr. Fixit in their remarkably-run home, where he pounces upon any request she might make. Tinkers in his garage.

When you define a person as a friend you may mean he or she is an acquaintance. Someone you like to be around and who seems to like you. Or you may also mean one who walks with you, stays by your side. One who steadies you as you make your way through seemingly impassable patches.

Paul hears that the young teenage son of a friend has taken his own life. He goes immediately to sit with him. Cry with him. To let him know that he feels his pain. Paul acts out his prayers for this single father in the ensuing days, months and years. He is faithful to and present with him in his long journey through the darkness.

A pilot has died in a tragic fall off a mountain. Paul and Carmen go to console the widow and to offer help. They have been in close touch with her in the years that have passed since her husband's death. Always ready to assist her with both the small and big decisions she has needed to make as a single mother.

My son and his wife, friends who reach out to others even before they ask for help. Paul understands what it means to feel different. Isolated. And in pain. That life sometimes demands extraordinary patience, courage and self-discipline.

During this past year of pandemic isolation, my phone rings every day at some point before the dinner hour. The sound of Paul's voice, even and calm, lifts me up. This is not a duty call. Paul is not in a hurry. He wants to hear his mom's voice. All the details of my day, however mundane. He is a sounding board for the decisions I need to make on a daily basis.

Today, I see Paul, in his sixties, the little Mr. Fixit grown into an exceptional human being. A guy with a heart. Gentle, with strong shoulders to lean on. And, like his Dad, always a tool box at the ready.

I am certain that a little boy called Sandy would have liked to visit Leonardo's workshop.

Perhaps share ideas about how to build a robot. Or an airplane. Or most importantly, a good life.

18.
ENOUGH IS
ENOUGH

IN THE EARLY SPRING of 1965 we buy a house on Point Loma in San Diego. The Vietnam war is raging. This means that Oscar has to report for duty on a destroyer headed for the Gulf of Tonkin. Its mission is to support the troops ashore and to ensure the safe transfer of troops, pilots, and ships at sea in the war zone. Oscar's ship leaves for training just a few days after our household goods arrive. I am left alone to settle our children, Laura Joy, seven, and Sandy, five, in their new home and school. The ship arrives home six weeks later, ready to deploy. In short order, I find myself standing on the pier, kissing him goodbye. Watching his ship disappear over the horizon, knowing that it will be many months before I will see it return.

Oscar makes four trips to Vietnam over this five year period. He serves on two destroyers, first as executive officer of the USS *Hoel* (DDG-13) and then as commanding officer of the USS *Wiltsie* (DD-716.) Each back-to-back trip means an absence of from 8–10 months. If we are lucky, his ship will be docked in San Diego for a few months before leaving again for training and deployment.

While our men are fighting a war abroad, we Navy

wives at home are fighting, too. Letters take several months to travel back and forth. With my family 2,000 miles away in Minnesota, I have to rely on myself to make wise decisions, to take proper care of the children, cope with broken bones, pneumonia, surgeries, fevers. To deal with the sudden death of Oscar's mother.

The loneliness.

Friends marvel at how calmly I face these challenges. How did I find the strength to get through the endless days and months?

February 1968. Oscar is about to leave on his fourth consecutive trip to Vietnam. Something begins to change within me. I have covered myself in a wall of pride. I am so brave, so strong, and so proud of the way I handle these long separations. The wall is beginning to crack.

Several friends come to stand with me as Oscar's ship passes over the horizon. I try to be brave, but I cannot control my emotions. I am near the point of collapse. This shouldn't be happening to me. Not again! Marilyn takes me in her arms. Holds me. She and Bob, as civilians, have never understood until this moment what it feels like to be the one who must stand alone, waving goodbye. They take me to lunch and then to the afternoon Bible class. The reading is First Corinthians, Chapter Thirteen: "Love doesn't boast, love is patient, kind. Love endures all things…"

Afterward, at home, I open my Bible and reread it. And am hollow. Beaten down. Angry. I slam my Bible down on the table. Hard.

God, I did it. For three years I did it. I was strong. I endured. But I don't have any strength left.

I am empty.

I don't have YOUR kind of love.

ENOUGH IS ENOUGH!

Laura Joy and Sandy come home from school to find me crying. Laura Joy gives me her handkerchief to wipe my tears. Sandy cuddles up to me. They miss their Daddy, too.

It takes a few days, awful days of self-pity, before my mind rearranges itself. I am on the wrong track. This isn't about me. I turn my thoughts to Oscar and his shipmates, who are in harm's way, sacrificing their lives with their families to serve a greater cause.

I think about our children and the children of the ship's crew. They will miss their fathers' arms around them in the happy and not so happy times ahead.

I think of the young wives who are left behind to face the unknown, alone. I am the captain's wife. They look to me for courage and strength. I think about how I might find ways to reach out to them. To be available to help when help is needed.

To love all of them with the love I had read about in that Bible study. God's love.

In that love I will find my strength. It had gone missing. But only temporarily.

I roll up my sleeves. Go into the kitchen to bake some Angel Cookies. My kids' favorites.

19.

A TRIP TO
THE HOSPITAL

SEVEN A.M. NOVEMBER 1, 1971. It is a bright autumn morning at #3 Lorre Court, Rockville, Maryland. There is a stillness in the air. The quiet that comes after the shrieks and laughter of neighborhood children ringing doorbells and gathering too many sugary treats. As I open the front door to retrieve The Washington Post from a significant pile of oak leaves, golden, red and brown, glittering in the sunlight, I collide face to face with a skeleton. It is twelve-year-old Sandy's creation, unfocused eyes dripping blood above green slimy teeth, designed to scare even the most brave. Last night's Halloween celebration has now become a memory. Big sister Laura, at fourteen, had joined her brother in taking charge of the festivities, happily decorating, creating costumes, getting bags and bags of candies ready for the streams of children who would soon be at our door.

Now it is time to get back to our normal routine. To take a warm bath and get some rest. I take a deep breath. Take in the spicy fragrance of fall, soothing and renewing. No wonder I am feeling unusually tired. After all, I am thirty-nine and close to nine months pregnant.

8 a.m. Daddy has eaten his Wheaties, gulped his coffee

and set off in his green Volkswagen Beetle for work at the Navy buildings in Arlington. Laura and Sandy have dragged themselves into our '50s pink kitchen—pink walls, pink fridge, pink dishwasher, pink towels. You get the idea. Too much candy and too much pink. They pick at their breakfast and go to their bedrooms to dress for school.

I should mention that Laura and Sandy are in a high state of excitement at the approaching entrance of a new brother or sister. I have promised the kids that they will accompany me to the hospital if I deliver while Dad is at work and unable to make it in time. They are ready to step into his shoes. I noticed during evening prayers that Sandy had laid out his shoes with socks in them, underwear, jeans and shirt on the floor beside his bed. Laura, downstairs in the privacy of her bedroom, I fear, was not about to decide in advance what fashion statement she was going to make on any given day.

As for me, I go up to my bedroom to dress before driving them to school. At that moment, as I try to bend down over my huge tummy to put on my loafers, all plans for a restful day go poof.

My water has broken. A sharp pain follows. Then another.

"Laura! Sandy! It's Time! Hurry!"

I stagger to the phone, leave a message for Oscar to come to the hospital. Laura, meanwhile, has actually dressed and is ready to go, along with Sandy, who stands by my side. Frozen. Eyes open wide. Staring at me. At my belly. Obviously worried about what he will do if he has to deliver the baby.

Clothes on. Now, how to get to the hospital?

Laura screams, "Call Mr. Mealy!"

Good idea, if he hasn't already left to take the five little

Mealys to school. Laura phones the Mealys, who live next door. Mother Sybil says they are out front getting into the station wagon. Joe Mealy parks the station wagon loaded with the five little Mealys in front of our house, assesses my condition with his well-practiced look, grabs me by what is left of my waist, stuffs me into the front seat, and guns the engine.

Rush hour on the Rockville Pike. An unbroken chain of cars stretching from the northern suburbs to Washington, D.C., moving at a snail's pace. The pains are coming every few minutes. I am too busy trying to breathe to even think of timing them. All eyes are on me, the seven kids in the back seats screaming every time I stiffen and groan with the pains. Joe remains calm as he moves through the heavy traffic, eying me, leaning on his horn, ignoring the returning serenade of honks as he blazes through red lights.

9 a.m. Good job, Joe! You got us to the hospital safely. You screech to a halt at the entrance, rush around to get me into the door. During which time the seven kids escape from the car and into the hospital.

Heads shaking at the sight of seven children trailing a seriously pregnant in-a-hurry mother.

12:36 p.m. Our little angel has arrived. Dad is present. Toes and fingers counted. A line of nurses and doctors coo over his shoulder-length mass of golden hair. Soon our family is reunited in the elevator, where Laura and Sandy meet their little brother. Sandy tapes the voice of the nurse as she cuddles our baby and says, "Welcome to the World."

20.
EKKIE

1971. BABY ERIK came as a blessing to his mother, father and a sister and brother who were in their teens and regarded themselves as a second set of parents. Erik thought it was normal to grow up with four parents. There was Mama, Daddy, and the teenagers—Oogie and Paul. Baby Erik couldn't say Laura, but she answered to his "Oogie." And he answered to "Ekkie."

While Mom and Dad are busy with adult things, the teens are entertaining Ekkie. He likes to be walked up the stairs in the split level. Like his siblings, he learns to walk by nine months. Probably due to all those exercises on the stairs. Or maybe to make a getaway from all that attention.

With the teens well-trained in keeping baby safe, Oscar and I decide to entrust Oogie and Paul with his care while we go out on a date. Arriving home, we notice that the picture window in the family room is boarded up. Our neighbor, Joe, is standing beside it. Smirking. Oogie had thrown the heavy Washington, D.C. telephone book at the window in an effort to dispose of a pesky housefly. The good news is that she missed the baby.

When Ekkie turns three years old, the teens are busy with high school activities. That leaves Ekkie on his own. He begins a new hobby: costumes. Cowboy, fireman, Batman, Robin, Superman, ghost, policeman, spaceman. He wears only costumes. Exclusively. He changes them many times a day.

With all those costumes handy, Ekkie decides that he will be Batman at Halloween. Since Daddy will be a 6-foot-3 inch Robin to a 3-foot Batman, we suggest that they switch roles. No. Ekkie is adamant. So, I come up with a suitable Robin costume for Daddy. It consists of his long winter underwear, his olive swim trunks and an "R" across his tee shirt. Off the famous duo goes, a reluctant Daddy in his underwear, to trick or treat in our neighborhood.

That includes the residence of a very dignified Admiral.

Who laughs so raucously I hear him at our house a block away.

As Erik's mom, I saw his love for literature and writing blossom during his high school years. He always had a book close at hand. He chose English as his major when he entered Trinity University in San Antonio, largely, he said, to avoid spending too much time on numbers. The highlight of his freshman year was a conversation with John Updike, who had come to the campus to talk about his books.

Erik is encouraged by the faculty to pursue a path in writing. He does, but in his own way. Erik has found another passion. With his high school guitar in hand, he starts a band, is soon composing the lyrics and music. Songs that uplift. Songs that tell a story. Songs that make you ponder. Rock and folk rock and soft ballads. The band is a campus favorite. Grammy winner guitarist Joe Reyes and Odie Cole have partnered with Erik for the past 20 plus years, the three of them coming up with innovative ideas for musical performances. Their band, Buttercup, is based in San Antonio. Several times a year, with Erik as MC, Buttercup and Joe and Erik's side project,

Demitasse, perform at San Antonio's Tobin Performing Arts Center, downtown theaters and the Riverwalk with a crowd of longtime fans.

It's been a long journey with the band.

After graduation, Erik begins to teach college admission prep courses for high school students. Erik is aware that students learn best from teachers who capture their attention. Who step into their shoes in order to engage them in the learning process. In time, he realizes that he can use the skills he has honed on stage with the band as a master of ceremonies, as an entertainer, to engage his students in the learning process.

Erik carries a sort of Scandinavian slant in his eye, a humorous half-wink, a pursing of his lips, that draws you in to hear what he is about to say.

His bank of knowledge is endless and timely. He has taught classes at Texas universities and high schools and tutored hundreds of students privately for almost 30 years. He is a forever student. One who delights in sharing what he has learned with his students.

Erik is happy about the success of his work with low income, at-risk kids who are the first in their family to go to college. For years he has spent many of his Saturday mornings teaching this under-served demographic. Thrilling when they get that college acceptance letter.

It is a snowy March evening. Erik's brother, Paul, has just married Carmen in a surprise wedding before a group of friends. They are in a yurt atop a Park City, Utah mountain. Erik's toast to the bride and groom brings an unforgettable ending to the evening. Strumming his guitar, he wanders around the room, heads toward the bride and groom, eyes them, singing his song, *I Love You.* A song with three simple words. Three simple words, sung three times. Then, he turns his back on them as if to leave. Seems to change his mind about leaving, turns back to them, repeating, *I Love You, I Love You, I Love You.* Just those three words, growing in passion. Just those three words, over and over again. Ad infinitum.

Where is this going? Where is the rest of the song?

Then, it dawns on us. *I Love You.* This is the beginning, the middle, and the ending.

Laughter builds. Explodes into cheers. Tears flow.

A perfect performance.

A perfect ending to a perfect evening.

21.
THE LOST
TRUMPET

"Palaces to shacks, shacks to palaces," one seasoned wife tells me as our family leaves our lovely home to stay in a WWII quonset hut in a Navy shipyard. This isn't exactly the place the kids and I would choose to spend our summer vacation. But, my Navy commander husband, Oscar, has orders to move his ship to the shipyard to be refitted before deploying to Vietnam. Once the ship leaves the shipyard, Oscar will be gone for many months. Our time together as a family is precious. We will go to the shipyard to be with him while we can. I am feeling sad to think that the trip to Grandma and Grandpa's lake house in Minnesota will have to be postponed for another year.

"You promised we could go see Grandma and Grandpa." Laura, nine, and Paul, seven, are feeling sad, too.

The kids are too young to understand that when the admiral orders Dad to go, he needs to go. The Admiral counts on me, as a military wife, to support his officer in all ways possible. No matter how difficult it may be.

Sometimes I sigh for a more ordinary life.

The quonset hut… We make it an adventure.

"How would you like to live next to Dad's ship? He will

take you deep down inside it to the engine room, where nobody else gets to go."

Paul, "WOW!"

"How would you like to live in a crazy house where the ceiling is on the floor?"

Laura, "NEAT!"

And I find myself caught up in their enthusiasm.

Our two month's stay at the Mare Island, California Naval Shipyard quonset hut ranks far above a vacation in an elegant hotel. Our children have the run of the naval base. The sailors play ball with them. Look out for them as they play in the streets. Show them how to line up in formation and march.

The steam horn blasts us out of our cots every night at midnight.

"COOL!"

Our family comes away with a valuable history lesson. Life in a quonset hut is confining. It is a corrugated steel cage. Your head gets bumped if you walk too close to the outer edges, where the semi-cylindrical ceiling meets the floor. The bedrooms are just big enough to hold a cot and a tiny chest. The decor is stark. Dull beige. For our family, living in a quonset is a novelty. For many Japanese families of the 1940s, it was a prison. And they couldn't go home after the summer.

Our family begins to move around the country for numerous tours of shore duty. From 1969 to 1981, we move from San Diego to Washington, D.C. to Norfolk, Virginia, back to Washington, then to Charleston, South Carolina.

The children grow up learning to adapt to new homes, schools, churches, and surroundings. They grow up knowing what it is like to be the new kid on the block. They learn how to make new friends. To choose strength rather than weakness. Our sense of family is intense. We are in this together. When the moving van takes off with our possessions, we pile into the car to follow it to our new home. We sing the miles away. Excitement builds as we begin another adventure.

Our family develops a philosophy, an attitude toward life that serves us well throughout our lifetimes. Life is a series of adventures. Most happy. Some painful. Many are temporary. Look for the good things in the bad.

* * *

1976. Oscar, now a Captain, has orders. We will be moving from Norfolk to the Washington, D.C. area. He will be program manager and controller of Sea Sparrow, a joint NATO venture to design, produce and install guided missiles on destroyers. Oscar will be taking on a tremendous responsibility. He will be working with NATO and the navies of seven European countries.

The moving van is pulling out of our driveway. It is scheduled to deliver our household goods at our new home in Alexandria in five days. We load our car with a few necessities, the kids screaming "Goodbye, House!" We drive at top speed to Alexandria. There is nothing like the noise of kids dashing around an empty house to lay claim to their own spaces. A mom visualizing her family gathering around the ancient kitchen table for supper. The dad down in the quiet of the basement plotting the layout of his workshop.

We are a family, all of us, looking forward to a new chapter. All but one.

Paul is silent. He does not join in the laughter and cries of pleasure from his sister and brother as they run around to discover each corner and nook of this house they are quick to call home.

Paul is not happy. He goes into his new bedroom and closes the door.

Paul is suffering. His parents have done the unforgivable. Paul will not be graduating with his classmates. He will no longer pal with his friends. Paul will be in a new home, new city, and a new school for his senior year.

He will no longer be playing his trumpet in the high school band.

We all remember the night that Paul's talent for music brought the fans to a glorious moment at the opening of the Tidewater Sharks hockey game in Norfolk...

Paul, in his white band uniform, stood tall, raised his trumpet to his lips and played *The Star Spangled Banner*. His trumpet, shining gold in the spotlight, overpowered the still air of the arena. Its clear silver tones moved like lightning, taking up every molecule of space from the floor to the rafters. The crowd exploded in cheers.

How can we even think of taking him away from his music teacher and his band? His senior year in high school?

Paul understands that a plan for Mom and the kids to live apart from Dad for an entire year is not a good one. Paul, as the son of a sea-going officer, spent nine of his growing up years with a largely-absent father. He knows what it means to grow up too fast because people pat him on the head and tell him 'now you are the man of the house.' He knows the tight feeling in his stomach when he sees the dads of his friends cheering them on at ball games. He knows how it feels to worry. Worry that he is forgetting his Dad's face. The sound of his voice.

The children need their father, and my husband and I need each other.

This is one of the hardest decisions Oscar and I have had to make.

With Paul's reluctant assent, we decide that Team Sanden has been through enough separations. We need to be together.

Here we are, in the new house. But Paul is not happy.

When the Navy loses our furniture, we try to maintain our spirit of adventure. We are living on Navy issue beds, a table, six chairs, some pots, pans and dishes. At first our family enjoys the idea that we are on a camping trip. After six weeks, we are getting grouchy. Crying for the familiar things that make a house a home. Like closets and chests full of coats, clothes, shoes and socks. Cupboards full of china, tablecloths, kitchen utensils, recipe books. Bicycles. The piano. Toys. Carpets for the bare floors. Pictures to go on the empty walls.

Our lives are on hold. We are stuck in a barren world.

Paul is losing patience. All our furniture is lost. His trumpet is lost. PAUL WANTS HIS TRUMPET. NOW! He asks his dad to take him to Cameron Station, the military household goods warehouse just a few miles to the west. We are told repeatedly that our furniture has not arrived. Location unknown. Paul decides to look for himself. It takes several hours to walk through the station. It is the size of several football fields.

Paul finds his trumpet. Paul finds our furniture.

Except for the ironing board and a few other necessities which are later located in Venezuela.

Later that evening, our family celebrates Paul, our hero. Paul wears a big grin as we toast him. He has taken charge of a family crisis like a man. He has found our furniture. He has found his trumpet. I sense that Paul has discovered a strength, an outlook that will help him to quickly move beyond the painful moments that come from being the new kid on the block.

On the first day of his senior year in high school, on foreign soil, Paul carries his trumpet.

Paul carries his trumpet, proudly, like a knight bearing his sword.

Across the green grass. Into the battle.

Paul carries his trumpet up the steep granite steps of his new school.

12 steps. Count them.

Paul opens the door. Heads straight for the band room.

Makes some music with his new friends.

22.
FLYING HIGH

I HAVE NEVER FLOWN alone on an overseas flight. I am feeling quite worldly. A trip to Denmark, where my Navy husband will meet with NATO while I explore the magic of Copenhagen with the other Navy wives.

Oscar has already left for Copenhagen, with a stop in Oslo. I am about to leave for Dulles to board an overnight flight. Oscar will meet me at the hotel tomorrow night.

I am in the bedroom fighting with my suitcase. It is overloaded with carefully-chosen outfits for numerous receptions and formal dinners. For a brief moment I worry that something could go wrong on the trip. And I alone would need to set things straight. Oscar, always calm, dealt with problems, big or small.

The phone rings. It is Finn Andersen, calling from Copenhagen. Finn is one of the Danish naval officers assigned to Oscar's office in Washington.

"Lila, Captain Sanden has told me you are flying alone to Copenhagen. I would like to meet your plane and deliver you to the hotel."

Mistake #1:

I say, "Thank you, Finn, but I can manage fine. My plane

won't get in until 4 a.m. your time. I'll just get a taxi to the hotel, go to my room and take a long nap."

We are seated two in a row on the flight. An elegant salmon dinner has been served, topped off with a tray of Danish chocolates. It is midnight. I have been dozing. The plane is dark except for tiny lights at floor level. My seat mate is snoring. Everyone is asleep, except the flight attendant and I. She appears to be reading a book, in the light of a little glass cabin about a city block down the aisle.

Mistake #2:

I forgot to remember that our friends no longer invite me to sail because I routinely get seasick and throw up all over their boats. I forgot to keep my motion sickness pills handy. I forgot that I had taken a pill before I put the bottle into my carry-on and stowed it high above in the luggage bin. I know the signs. I am dizzy. I try to stand, but I can't get my balance. I am about to pass out! I ring for the flight attendant, who comes, gets my bag down, hands me some water, and leaves me to take my pill.

Mistake #3:

I swallow the pill. Or was it a couple of pills? I am groggy and confused. Desperate. I think I may have swallowed two pills instead of the prescribed one, but I am not sure. The next thing I know is that I am awakening to an empty plane. We have arrived in Copenhagen. All the passengers have left. I am alone. Drugged. So drugged that it takes two men to escort me off the plane. They leave me to stagger on my own the rest of the way. I need kroner to pay the cab driver. Not only can I not ask directions in Danish, I can't speak without slurring. I get the kroner by pointing; the same for the taxi.

It is 5 a.m. The reception desk at the hotel is closed. I see a bar with a human being behind it. Make my way over. He speaks English. Tells me my room won't be ready until noon. My eyes won't focus. I am fighting the need to lie down. I put my head down on the counter. He brings me black coffee. I drink it. Put my head down on the counter. He brings me another cup of coffee. I drink it. Put my head down on the counter. More coffee. I drink it. Put my head down on the counter…

It is now 7 a.m. My brain is starting to work. Call Sid! Sid is a civilian member of the Sea Sparrow staff staying in the hotel. Sid and his coworker, Robert, come to rescue me. They scoop me up, stuff me into an elevator, into Sid's room. Where the bed lies high up in a loft. Heaven must be lower.

Getting me up the steep ladder is difficult because my legs are rubber and my rescuers are busy laughing.

Eight hours later I emerge from a nap. The first reception of the NATO meeting is well underway when I enter the crowded, noisy room filled with Navy brass and civilian CEOs. An abrupt silence envelopes the room. All eyes turn on me, and then the entire group explodes into laughter.

Obviously, they have heard all about the arrival and outrageous behavior of one particular Navy wife.

23.
DON'T GIVE UP
THE SHIP

1980. CHARLESTON IS AS colorful in the fall as it is in summer. Here, at Quarters A, the gardens surrounding our aged plantation house are in full bloom. The hibiscus, called confederate rose in these parts, dazzles the eye with its mass of pink, white and lavender flowers resting high above the earth on thick shrubs of forest green. Canna lilies, reds, oranges and yellows, greet the morning sun. I step out from under the *porte cochere* to capture the sight of my menfolk leaving for the day. Erik, to the base primary school, and his dad to his office. Oscar, tall and erect in his white uniform, reaches down, tousles Erik's yellow hair, takes his hand as they walk down the narrow lane under the shade of the bordering live oaks.

I say a prayer of thanks for the beauty of this day.

Back in the house, I marvel at the good fortune that has brought us to this magical place, the largest naval base in the country. Over 10,000 families—in addition to an unknown number of civilian staff, Naval personnel, Submariners, Marines, Seals, among them—all living on the Naval Weapons Station and land spread over North Charleston. Miles and miles of woods and grassy areas cover the land. Countless ponds and streams are home to alligators who like to roam the streets.

Oscar, at forty-eight, is the commanding officer.

Our house fronts on the Cooper River. I take my morning coffee out to the bench under the giant magnolia, as I often do, to watch the river. A small boat takes its time to float up the river. The sun dances, shimmers, as it meets the blue-green waters. I bask in the peace of this morning.

I hear a car, brakes squealing. An officer hurries across the grass to give me a message.

At that moment, the magic disappears.

"The Captain has been taken down to the Naval Hospital by ambulance. He became ill while in the middle of a lecture."

Taken by ambulance? My heart starts to race. "What happened?" I ask.

"I don't know, Ma'am. But they took him down to Charleston, to the hospital."

Oscar could be dying. I am having trouble breathing, and my mind won't tell me what to do. Erik! I need to call Barbara, our neighbor. Ask her to keep an eye out for Erik. I may not be here when he arrives home from school. Then, I grab my purse and am in the car, speeding down the highway, praying.

A young sailor is standing by the door when I enter the hospital. The receptionist approaches me, says, "Mrs. Sanden, Seaman Roberts will escort you to the Commander's office."

Why are they taking me to the Commander? This isn't good. What has happened to Oscar? I feel like an actor playing a role on stage, not having seen a word of the script. This isn't real. I have to find Oscar. I start running, moving ahead of the sailor. He takes my arm and gently slows me down.

The Commander rises from his desk to greet me. He

wastes no time in seating me.

"First off, I want you to know how sorry I am to tell you that the Captain has suffered a stroke."

I swallow hard. There seems to be a big lump in my throat.

"The neurology team is watching him closely. This is a critical time. If all goes well, they expect the outcome to be good."

Okay, I think. Okay. He has survived a stroke. Funny, to feel such relief at the news your husband has had a stroke.

He tells me that he is sending me over to the ICU, where Oscar is being treated. The doctor will talk with me, answer any questions I might have.

"This is going to be a long, difficult time for you," he warns. "You will be an essential part of his treatment. You will be spending a good deal of time here. Should you have any concerns, if you want to talk, please know that I am your friend, and here to help you."

The Commander has calmed me with his kind words. But not enough to deter me from rushing out the door, where the seaman waits to take me to the ICU.

The ICU is a busy, noisy place with all sorts of machines running and nurses and doctors moving about. The nurse is expecting me. Before I can locate Oscar's bed, a doctor guides me into a tiny office. He introduces himself as the neurologist charged with the care of my husband. The nurse brings me coffee and water. I wave them aside. "Where is my husband?" I am losing patience. "Exactly what happened to him?"

He tells me that Captain Sanden was in the Station's auditorium giving a lecture. As he wrote on a board, he dropped the chalk. He couldn't find his words. He began to slur. He lost his balance. Thankfully, a sailor caught him as he fell. The base ambulance arrived in three minutes, brought him here, and it was determined that he had suffered a stroke. He has reduced sensation on the left side of his body. This would indicate that the stroke was caused by a bleed in his thalamus. A hemorrhagic stroke. Most strokes are caused by blood clots. His, by bleeding in the brain.

"There are several things you should know before you see him. His condition is serious. We need to verify the diagnosis of a hemorrhagic stroke so we can continue treatment. We do not have the equipment here in Charleston to rule out other causes and to make a firm diagnosis. Early tomorrow morning, we are sending Captain Sanden to Portsmouth Naval Hospital for a cat scan and other tests. We are arranging for a medevac, a helicopter fitted like an ambulance, to take him. You and a medic will accompany him."

The doctor cautions me to prepare to be shocked when I see how helpless my big, strong husband looks today. I must try to remember that with therapy, rest and some luck, he will get better.

The neurologist takes me over to Oscar's bed. He is hooked up to a heart monitor and an IV. His eyes are closed. He seems to be in a deep sleep. How pale he is! I take his hand, but he doesn't stir. I lean down and say, "It's me, Sweetheart." His eyes flicker, but they don't open. He knows me. He is trying to speak, but sounds, not words, come out of his mouth.

This can't be. My heart is breaking. I turn away to hide my tears.

The doctor moves me to a quiet corner. Takes my hand.

"I have treated a number of stroke patients and most have recovered to lead full and long lives."

He tells me to go home and take care of my son.

How do you tell a little boy, just turning eight, that his father is critically ill? When Barbara brings Erik home, I decide to spare him the details of his father's illness. Still, talk of the Captain's stroke will be all over the base. Erik needs to know the situation from me. I tell him that Daddy got sick and had to take an ambulance ride to the hospital.

"Is Daddy going to die?" He looks up at me with tears in his blue eyes. I pull him toward me in a big hug.

"No, Daddy isn't going to die. But he will be feeling weak when he comes home."

"Where is Daddy now? I want to see my Daddy!"

"Daddy is resting at the hospital. Tomorrow morning, he and I will take a helicopter ride to Portsmouth Hospital. They have a cat scan machine that is like a computer with a camera. It will look into Daddy's brain to see if something there made him sick. I need to go with Daddy to help take care of him."

He frowns when I tell him that he cannot go with us. He agrees that he mustn't miss school. It is best that he stay at Barbara's.

Early the next morning I drop Erik off at Barbara's before I head to the airport.

"Tell Daddy that I love him a bushel and a peck," he shouts over his shoulder, as Barbara takes him in for breakfast.

Bushel and a peck, the words to Daddy's bedtime song. Erik may be a little boy, but he knows how to bring a smile to his father.

The week at Portsmouth Hospital is the worst and

longest week of my life. It passes in a blur, a kaleidoscope of doctors, friends who come to sit with me, to wait for seemingly endless hours, phone calls from family and friends who are praying from great distances. Mary Jane, a close Navy friend, loans me her car, sees that I get dinner and some needed rest in her guest room. Finally, at the end of the week, the neurologists confirm the original diagnosis: a hemorrhagic stroke. A tiny vessel in the right thalamus of Oscar's brain has bled, causing pressure on the organs that control motion and balance. His left side is numb and weak. He needs assistance when walking. His tongue is numb. His speech is slurred.

Surgery is not an option. There could be another, possibly fatal, bleed at any time. Or not. The doctors cannot predict an outcome. It is a wait-and-see situation. We are heartened to hear that a patient with an identical history lived 20 years after his stroke.

His mind has not suffered. Tests reveal that he is more than sharp. The psychologist offers to recommend him to Mensa. Oscar has only one thought. Survival.

We return home to begin the long journey to recovery. To face the truth and make the painful decisions that we need to make. Oscar can no longer carry out his duties as commanding officer. We will vacate our quarters at the Weapons Station as soon as he is able to travel. We need to get up to Washington, to the Naval Hospital, where he will receive the best care possible.

After several months of therapy, his doctors declare him strong enough to travel. He is gaining strength and walking with the aid of a cane. We are feeling great relief at his progress. But we are sinking into a deep, dark pool of sadness. As we pack our belongings into boxes, we are packing away a wonderful life.

Sealing it away forever.

Oscar withdraws into silence. He is losing his identity as a proud, able team member of his beloved Navy. He does not share this with me, but I feel his sorrow.

We worry about Erik. He is trying to be brave, but his eyes betray an abiding fear.

"What if my Dad gets really sick again? Can't we just stay here so I can be in my school with my friends?"

"Why don't my friends come to play with me anymore?"

Yes, that adds to the hurt. Except for the Chaplain, the Admiral, his doctor, and a few fellow officers who come to visit, we are alone in this house. Friends and neighbors stay away. They mean well, I am sure, but, though it sounds unreasonable, I am beginning to feel a sense of shame. As if we are being shunned for some failure of our own. It is a deep, hurtful feeling.

One evening, hearing a noise, I open the door to see a tub of ice cream melting on the porch. White vanilla-flavored ice cream, melting, running down our front steps.

Melting away. Like our lives.

"Why didn't our neighbor ring the bell and come in to talk with us?"

We pack up and slip away to Maryland, flee to the open arms of Bob and Donna, our longtime close friends. Bob and Donna go far beyond the duties of friendship. They give us their guest room, store our furniture in their Potomac garage, and are there for us as we face the unknown. We gain strength and hope just by being in their presence.

Weeks go by. Oscar spends hours each day in therapy. He is slowly regaining strength and some feeling. He is able to walk a good distance with a cane. Born left-handed, he is learning to use his right hand to write, eat, lift. He is working hard to speak clearly, as he cannot feel the left side of his tongue.

He has difficulty saying my name. I overhear him practicing, "Lila...Lila...Lila..." behind closed doors.

I must not let him see my tears.

Oscar is a brave man. He will encounter his illness squarely. Just as he faced threatening situations in the past:

1962. Oscar was weapons officer on the USS *Sellers*, a guided missile destroyer. A live explosive was jammed in a gun mount, hot wires hanging out. An explosion was imminent. The entire ship's crew stopped breathing. High on the bridge the captain looked down in silence. No one spoke. No one moved. All eyes were on Oscar. He stepped forward, ever so slowly edged the explosive out of the gun mount. Carried it above his head, like a waiter balancing a loaded tray of fragile china. He moved slowly, step by step, to the side of the ship. Threw it out to the sea.

He came home that night. I asked him how his day went. "Oh, the usual," he said.

Oscar has a pillow embroidered with the final command that Captain James Lawrence of the USS *Chesapeake* gave on June 1, 1813: "Don't give up the ship."

Oscar is not going to give up.

This is not the end of his life.

This is the beginning of a new chapter.

24.

THE SWEDES ON
THE HILL

Spring 1981. Our family has no home. Oscar, Erik and I are staying with our friends, Donna and Bob, in close range of Bethesda Naval Hospital in Washington. Oscar is an outpatient, in a slow recovery from the stroke that led to his retirement after 28 years in the Navy. The Mecklenburgs have done wonders for us in their efforts to provide a sense of normalcy to our visit. Still, Oscar cannot hide the sadness he feels, not only at the loss of his good health, but the abrupt end to his Naval career. The Oscar we all know as an outgoing, most interesting conversationalist has turned quiet.

Erik has turned quiet, too. Like his Dad.

"We might as well expect that I will have another stroke at any time. And that will be the end." This is how Oscar feels.

"There is no hope," he says.

"I'm going to die and you're going to be a rich widow."

A failed attempt at a joke. Oscar isn't joking. He tells me this and then he retreats into his own solitary world of despair.

Oscar's sighs are frequent and deep when I mention that we need to find a home. He closes his eyes. He is too weak to think of house hunting. But, fall is around the corner. Erik will need to enroll in a new school.

"Where would you like to live?"

I am thinking we might return to one of the many places we have lived during Oscar's service in the Navy.

Oscar responds, stone-faced, in a tone that says he can't be bothered by any questions I might have.

"Whatever you wish," he says.

Whatever I wish. This is the answer I hear, over and over. I tell him that I want to know how *he feels* about a decision.

"Whatever you wish," he mutters. Eyes closed.

And I am so sad at what he has become. I feel so alone.

And frustrated. I need his opinions on basic matters. I know Oscar is ill and depressed, but sometimes I feel that I will scream if I hear "Whatever you wish" one more time. I need help.

A pastor counsels me, "Be Joyful in hope, patient in affliction, faithful in prayer."

This is what I must do. I must fully believe in Oscar's recovery. He will feel my optimism. We will live each day as a gift, meant to be celebrated and used well. We will dwell on what we have and be thankful. There will be a return of Oscar's wonderful zest for life.

I must be mindful that the stroke has changed him. This isn't Oscar uttering those pitiful words. I must be understanding and patient, as I have never been before.

The stroke causes him to turn inward. He doesn't notice me when I enter a room. Now, I am just another person. I feel ugly.

I long for the day when he will look at me, his hazel eyes alight with love.

I long for the day when he will, as before, call me his

Sweetie Pie.

"We are going to lick this," I tell him, over and over, so many times that he begins to hear me.

"We need to fight this, and we are going to win."

One day, Oscar calls to me, "Lila, I want you to see this!"

And he climbs up a flight of stairs, unassisted, by himself. He is excited about this big step in his rehabilitation. I see a glimmer of hope in his eyes.

I decide that our family will benefit from some summer fun. We travel north to the town of Washington, Connecticut to visit Oscar's brother, John, his wife, Elizabeth, and their daughter, Pamela. Erik and his cousin know each other well. Pamela had stayed with our family for close to a year following the death of her mother, Priscilla, after a stroke. Pammy and Erik were babies at the time. They have remained close.

Oscar and I have never been in this part of Connecticut. Historic small towns with white wooden houses gleaming in the sunlight, buildings of aged red brick, dot the green countryside. We fall in love with the tiny town of Washington. Set in the southern foothills of the Berkshires, Washington was settled by colonists in the mid-1700s. It was initially a farming community. Swedish immigrants came toward the end of the 19th century, adding to the cultural mix.

The landscape of the town seems to dictate the culture. Washington is split in two by the Shepaug River. High above the river, Washington's town green is encircled by historic homes, each one a priceless example of colonial architecture. Episcopalians settled here, along with Congregationalists. A steep hill to the west of the green leads down to the river. Set in a small valley, Washington Depot is the other half of Washington.

It was once the terminus of the Shepaug River Valley Railroad. The tracks were removed in 1948, but this section of Washington continues to be known as the Depot. Most of the area's businesses are to be found here. Elizabeth and John are living in and renovating a house near the river.

John, Elizabeth and Pam are waiting outside their home to welcome us. Pam and Erik cannot contain their excitement at being together. Squealing with delight, they run off, hand in hand, into the sunshine.

Erik is a kid again.

Erik, Oscar and I take a tour of the Depot. It is no more than a mile wide, with a population of less than 1,000. The market, the bank, the post office and a number of stores seem to have everything one would need to keep a home going. The townspeople are friendly. Strangers are easily spotted. Several people stop to ask if we need help or just to chat about the weather. No one seems to be in a hurry. Time seems to move forward at a slow pace.

As we travel, Erik has been reading *The Lion, the Witch, and the Wardrobe,* one of seven books about Narnia, a fantasy land, by C. S. Lewis. We are touched at how deeply Erik responds to this beautifully written story. He wipes tears from his eyes when he reads about the senseless murder of Aslan, the pure and innocent lion.

Oscar stops to chat with an elderly man, white hair neatly trimmed, designer steel-rimmed glasses, checkered barn jacket and jeans straight out of Abercrombie and Fitch. He points out that the living here in Litchfield county is so good that a number of movie stars: Marilyn Monroe, Richard Widmark and Dustin Hoffman, have places here. And writers Frank McCourt, William

Styron and Arthur Miller, who remained here after he and Marilyn were divorced. Musical composer Stephen Sondheim lives down the road. Singer-songwriter James Taylor has a huge farm.

I stare at this handsome man. I wonder if he is one of the famous?

"Is there a bookstore?" Oscar asks. He wouldn't spend an hour in a town without a bookstore.

The old gentleman guides us to the Hickory Stick Bookshop. A goldmine of books, thousands of them, with pillowed nooks waiting for you to tuck in and read. We enter the bookshop. Erik goes directly to the children's section, sees a set of C. S. Lewis's Narnia books. A whole set! His eyes grow wide.

Erik would sleep here if he could.

"Mom, Dad, I want to live here, please, can we live here?" Erik pleads.

Oscar and I exchange a 'why not?' look.

Life is full of surprises. We came here on a visit. Now we are looking for a house.

While Oscar rests, Elizabeth and I meet Jeff Fairburn, contractor, and Butch, his carpenter. They show us a home in a neighboring town, a colonial style barn with a contemporary flair. The living room ceiling is open to the rafters, a full two stories above the floor. A loft, reminiscent of a hayloft, rises above the dining area. I am in a state of enchantment. Call me decisive or call me impulsive—I know that this is what we must have, a modern barn with a roof reaching up to the sky, waiting to capture the music of our lives. I tell Jeff that we need look no further for the design of our new home.

Jeff takes Elizabeth and me on a drive up the steep hill on the west side of the Depot. We pass a small Swedish Covenant church at the top of the hill, surrounded by narrow roads and neatly-kept homes.

"This is where the Swedes live," he says.

The town people call them "The Swedes on the hill."

Now, I am a believer in signs. A Swedish church for my Swedish Oscar! I grew up a Finn in Minneapolis, among Swedes, in a Swedish Lutheran church. This is where we will build our new home.

Our Barn.

"A barn? You want to live in a barn?" Oscar shakes his head at the idea that I want to build a barn for our next home.

"Have you lost your mind?"

Maybe so. But when I show him the plans for the house, he gets excited. When he hears of my plan to settle in a Swedish-American community, he is about to burst with enthusiasm. His father was born in Sweden, spoke the language fluently, as did most of his family.

Living with the Swedes on the hill will be like coming home.

I am beginning to think that this little trip to Washington has brought my husband back to me.

We have no problem selecting a site for the barn. Jeff takes us down a winding lane to a wooded lot—old oaks, birch, pine, and linden. The lot leads downhill to a tiny runoff. Perfect for a boy to roam with his friends.

* * *

Fall 1981. Work on the house is underway. Oscar leaves the shelter of Donna and Bob's home to join Erik and me at John and Elizabeth's, where we will stay until our house is ready.

Jeff tells us that our home will be finished by the end of the next summer. Erik has entered the fourth grade at the Shepaug school. He and Pamela, who is in the third grade, go off happily each morning to board the school bus.

We are deep into winter; the work has stopped. Oscar involves himself with the plans for the house, choosing materials. His old energy is coming back. We drive down to Yale University for doctor's visits.

We are warmly welcomed at the church. The Swedes on the hill have, over time, been assimilated, but the Swedish heritage of the congregation reveals itself in the number of Olsons, Petersons, Andersens and Carlsons. And through the singing of Swedish hymns and Scandinavian smörgåsbords.

Oscar and I delight in the music. I learn to make Swedish meatballs and *lefse* — Swedish flat bread — from the experts. *Lefse* is often served with meatballs. Our family likes it served warm with a topping of cinnamon and sugar.

Dee Goolsby, the choir director, and I become fast friends. We sing duets together in the church, and bring our music to senior homes around the state. Oscar finds a friend in Jim, Dee's pilot husband. Jim is a ray of sunshine. Oscar and Jim go off by themselves to talk engineering and planes while Dee, who was born of Filipino parents, cooks *Lumpia* — spring rolls made with pork, vegetables and a spicy sauce — and other dishes native to her family. Soon we are a part of their family.

Pastor David Sundell and his wife, LaVonne, open their home to us. David, soft-spoken and kind, is a source of strength for us during the time Oscar spends in recovery. He surprises us with his dry wit, a humorous raising of the eyebrows that turns a big problem into a little nuisance. LaVonne tosses her brunette hair, laughs, while confessing that her meatballs didn't pass the inspection by the smörgåsbord committee. This failure by the pastor's wife, no less, was probably well-noted by more than a few parishioners. She is happy to hear that I, too, had failed.

"LaVonne, you have what it takes to be a pastor's wife." Oscar admires—and has great empathy for—LaVonne. He is a PK—Pastor's Kid—whose halo often went askew. How refreshing it is, to be around someone who looks at life with a prevailing sense of humor.

Oscar and I often gather with the Sundells and the Goolsbys. On Saturday nights we tune in to Garrison Keillor's *A Prairie Home Companion* for a sweet dose of rural Minnesota nostalgia. Erik enjoys playing with his new friends, James and Drissing Goolsby, and Tim, the Sundell's son. We relax together at the church camp in New Hampshire.

These new friends bring our family to a present filled with health and happiness as a norm. We are leaving the sadness and fears of the past behind.

Erik begins piano lessons with Astrid, a retired teacher, who bears no nonsense from her students. Astrid, tall and strong of body, and her husband live on a hill in a tiny Swedish-style summer house—brown, with a bright red roof and white trim. Her blue eyes go soft when she tells me that she never has to remind or coax Erik to practice. Erik is serious about learning to play the piano. He has discovered that with dedicated work, he can make music. After a year and a half of concentrated effort, Erik, in a dark suit, sits at the baby grand piano in the church to play his first recital. He comes away, pleased with himself. He has managed to play a Schubert piece, not only without error, but with emotion.

Oscar and I are relieved to see that Erik no longer feels the anxiety that plagued him in the aftermath of Oscar's stroke. He has found a new life in this place. One of safety and happiness, within the bonds of family and friendships. And he has found music.

* * *

Summer 1982. Our Laura arrives for a summer break from the University of Minnesota Architecture School. She is as a novice carpenter working with Jeff and Butch on our house. A perfect summer job for an architecture student. She has made some valuable suggestions for the construction of the house. Now she will see them come to fruition.

Butch stops work to watch Laura, a left-hander, hit a bullseye with her left arm. She hits the nail again and again. The entire crew comes to see her perform. Laura, a female and a blonde, is now accepted by the all-male team.

Elizabeth and John have been so kind, sheltering us for well over a year. They have opened their hearts to us, sparing nothing in an effort to see Oscar through this trying time. Our home is now ready. Elizabeth and John will have their home back at last.

Our house is plank-sided in a soft gray, offset by white trim. It has three stories. A lower level with two bedrooms, an office and recreation room built into the hillside. A main level formal living-dining room with a loft and the high ceiling that drew me to the design. A kitchen open to a large family dining and entertainment area. An upper level with two bedrooms. All tied together by the dark hardwood flooring that flows throughout the house,

On a cool October morning, Oscar, Erik, and I bring our suitcases into our new home. Our Barn. The moving van, with all our furniture, is due to arrive within the hour.

We are watching for the van through the kitchen window when we see a vehicle coming down the road. We are surprised to see our son, Paul, step out of the car. Paul has driven from his Navy air base in Florida, unannounced, to do the muscle work his Dad can no longer do. Erik whoops at the sight of his big brother. Oscar and I wipe tears from our eyes. The thought that we have raised such a tender-hearted son overwhelms us.

There are moments in life that remain sealed in memory, destined to be opened and relived many decades later. It is of one of these moments that I write. As Erik rushes out to be scooped up by his brother, I stand at the door, giving thanks for our new home. A home at last. A place of love. At that moment, as I wait for my sons to enter, I am consumed by love. Love overflows my being. I will it to spill over everyone, Oscar, our family and friends, all who make this place a home.

"Welcome home, Paul," I say, as he pulls me into a hug.

* * *

1983. It is a cold winter Saturday. The thermometer outside our kitchen door registers at –30 degrees. We are making breakfast, our kitchen warm with the smell of bacon sizzling in the frying pan, hot pancakes and maple syrup ready to serve at the table. As we eat, Erik tells us that he would like to see the new *Star Wars* movie. It is too cold to play outdoors.

Oscar is in high spirits.

"Let's have a boy's day out, Erik. Just you and me. How about we go to New Milford, see the *Star Wars* movie, and then have a treat at the diner?"

Yes, Erik's Dad has come back. He no longer drives to Yale to see his neurologist. He is stable. He has learned to cope with his balance problem and numbness. Like a soldier, he has returned home with permanent wounds. Despite this, Oscar celebrates the life he's been dealt.

Friends question him about his stroke. Oscar says "I am one lucky fellow. And I intend to stay lucky for a long, long time."

How happy I am, to see him return to his old outgoing, affectionate self. I feel beautiful when he speaks to me; looks at me. I stand at the window to watch him walk into the forest with Erik. To see him go off to inspect the damage done to the oaks by the seven years visitation of the cicadas. To see him get down on his knees to work at odd jobs. He carries his heavy toolbox. He installs his radios in his basement ham shack. Humming as he works.

And I smile at what I hear and see.

* * *

February 1984. On Sunday mornings Oscar sits with Don Smith in a pew near the front of the church. Don is a retired vice president of the Singer Corporation. Oscar enjoys being around people who speak the language of mathematics, engineering and rocketry. Oscar comes alive when talking with Don. He becomes wistful when he speaks of his career in the Navy.

One Sunday morning, as the church empties after the

service, Don asks Oscar to stay a moment.

"Oscar, have you ever thought about going back to work?"

Oscar laughs, "No, who would have me, with my physical limits?"

Don responds, "We're talking here about your mind, Oscar. I believe you are just what the Singer Corporation wants. Nothing wrong inside that handsome head of yours, is there?"

Don continues, "There is a company in Glendale, California doing government work in the weapons industry. They are looking for a weapons specialist. Talk with Lila about this, and I will arrange an interview. You are just what they need. And I think you need them, too."

Several months later, we leave our beloved Swedes on the hill for the sunshine of Southern California.

25.

LISTEN TO THE
STILLNESS

IT IS STRANGE. The garage door is wide open as I pull into the driveway. I get out of the car, walk into the garage and find Oscar standing there, still as a statue, leaning over in the shadows. My eyes travel to his face. His hazel eyes seem to be focused on something far away. Then they find me. Oscar has something to tell me. And he tells me what I already know.

Oscar is worn down. 10 years have passed since a tiny vessel deep inside his brain had bled, leading to a right side paralysis and the end of his Navy career. He has taken a less stressful job in the weapons industry. Now, the paralysis is worsening and causing extreme fatigue. At fifty-eight, Oscar does not have the strength to work.

There in the garage, Oscar has come alone to think. To accept the hard truth. Listen to what his doctors are telling him. He should give up his job. Seek a peaceful life in retirement. Maybe leave the noises of the city. Slow down. Live quietly.

There in the garage, Oscar grieves as one grieves over the loss of a big space in his life.

The next morning we lay out a plan. We need healing. To find the joy that has gone missing.

We will sell the house, leave Glendale. Fill that empty space with the luxury of unhurried peace, quiet, new places, new adventures.

But where? We picture ourselves settling in a small town. Neighbors close by, houses row on row, cars and people moving about. Little cities with little strip malls sprouting up like weeds, bringing all the clatter of the big cities.

Out in the country, that's where we should go. A farm? Oscar can't handle the work. I am definitely not the farmer's-wife type. I like to get my eggs at the store.

Weeks go by as we struggle to find our little piece of paradise. Nothing rings a bell. Stress levels are high. We need to make a decision and move on it.

I think you may have heard that when you have been married to the same person for a long, long time you can read each other's mind. (This is not always a good thing.) So, it is no surprise that one day Oscar verbalizes just what I have been thinking.

"THE BOONDOCKS!" we yell, almost in unison.

A quick call to Herman, the world's best stepfather, and we have the green Explorer packed and rolling to the Boondocks, all the way up from Southern California to the North Shore of Lake Superior, at the very top of Minnesota.

The Boondocks, for many years a summer haven for our family. Herman had cleared a space in a heavily-forested lakeside lot, set well back from a country road. He had single-handedly cut down a stretch of spruce trees to create a narrow road to the clearing. Using tools from his workshop in Minneapolis, he transformed the trees into smooth exterior wall planks. The cabin was small, just one room, but it contained a galley kitchen, a stone fireplace with a sit-down hearth, a dining table, chairs, and a Murphy bed in an interior wall. An attached garage with a sleeping loft for the men—and the mice. An outhouse resided at a discreet distance, its interior walls plastered with old magazine photos of Hollywood glamour girls.

Once the last nail was hammered, Herman's little cabin on the shore of Lake Superior became a summer destination for over 40 years, for our family and anyone who called himself a relative or friend. I am sure that each visitor left with a store of happy memories. And a promise to return.

I remember long hikes through the woods, coming across cabins deep in the shelter of acre upon acre of giant firs, discovering old Indian trails, graveyards, hidden waterfalls. Canoing on inland lakes. Deer and moose spotting us, sometimes a bit too close. Visits to a French and Indian fur trading post. Trips across the nearby border to the Hoito, our favorite Finnish restaurant in the largely Finnish port city of Thunder Bay, Canada. Heavenly Finn pancakes—a dash of vanilla is the secret—topped with strawberries and whipped cream. Strong Finnish coffee.

We enjoyed the fruits of Herman's garden. Sweet, plump blueberries, rhubarb, tomatoes, summer squash.

The guys fished. A little stroll from the cabin down to the beach and then left to the rushing waters of the Brule river where trout, herring, salmon, and walleye moved fast. Once a year at midnight, a few of us ventured out with nets to capture smelt on their yearly run. Fried smelt, a fisherman's delight. Oscar, a city boy, came back to the cabin, forlorn, with just three miniature smelt in his net. Herman had a basketful.

We huddled over a bonfire in the chilly evenings to hear

tales of Herman's encounters with bears. Although a fervent hunter, he never fired his rifle on the property. He was known to ask Grandma Anna to make one of her Tabasco sandwiches for an ill-mannered bear who repeatedly made a mess while dining in the dark at the garbage can. One sandwich and he never came back.

Herman had met many a black bear on his walks through the woods. He did not fear them. Not since his WWII encounter with a Japanese sniper in a jungle on Leyte Island. The sniper, up a tree, pointed his rifle at Sergeant Olaf Herman Johanson, who was below in a clearing. Herman was looking for food for his starving young soldiers. Seems the two of them were hungry. Both had their eyes on the same wild pig. Herman just looked the young sniper in the eyes, made a "be my guest" gesture with his arms, turned his back on the sniper and walked away.

These were short summer visits, just enough to leave us with a hankering to get a real taste of what it might mean to live a simple life within the arms of Mother Nature.

But, we were city slickers. The Navy moved us 20 some times, most always to big cities. The idea of actually living in the woods had never crossed our minds.

Until this aforementioned trip.

Oscar and I join Herman and Mom at their home in Minneapolis for the last lap of our long journey from California to the cabin. It is April 1, spring in Minneapolis. As we make the six-hour drive straight north from the city to Duluth and finally to the cabin, we run into winter. The unpaved driveway is buried in newly-fallen snow. We have to shovel our way in.

The cabin is set on a strip of lake shore bordered by a river to the north and an inlet to the south. The six neighboring cabins on the shore are dark. Boarded up for the winter.

Not a single soul is about.

We get out of the car. Sink into a two-foot high drift.

Herman grins. Looks around, left, right, then whispers, "Nobody here! Can you hear the quiet?"

We stop…to listen…to the stillness…

Then, we slip into the cabin, our tiny group of four, to warm ourselves by a fire, cook a simple meal and visit. To just be in the moment.

In the morning, Oscar and I take a walk on a path through the woods. We come upon a brown plank-sided cabin set on the lakeside of three acres of wooded land, tall spruce, pines and aspen. It is a small wooden structure, 30 feet square, with a long wall-to-wall addition fronting the beach and the lake. Artists live here. That glassed-in front room is their studio.

We can't get inside. No one here. We peek in the windows. 1920s charm. Pot-bellied stove, a Norwegian *Jotyl*. A living-dining area big enough for a piano. A small kitchen, bedroom and bath.

We walk around the house to a wooden deck overlooking the lake. The beach, a bed of millions of rounded black rocks, and beyond, the blue waters of the Big Lake. The opposite shore is unseen, the horizon some 100 miles distant at Hancock, Michigan.

No houses in sight, only the lush green of trees, the endless blues of lake and sky. And blissful quiet. We breathe in the silence. Testing it. Listening for it.

This is no ordinary lake. This is an ocean. My Navy captain is silent, he gazes long and hard at the lake, hypnotized by its greatness and beauty.

His eyes send out sparks, as I had not seen them do since his illness overcame him. Tears wash over his face as he turns to me and says, "I could live here."

There is a for sale sign on the door.

Herman is honking the horn, impatient to leave for the city. So we drive back to California, take refuge in a Denver blizzard where Oscar, upon entering the motel, walks directly to the phone.

"Who are you calling?"

"I'm gonna buy that cabin."

"But we haven't been in it."

"What if I don't like it?"

"Then I'll build you a new one."

26.

CATHEDRAL ON
THE LAKE

IT HAS BEEN two years now that we have lived beside the lake. Our cabin sits just 40 feet from the water on a calm day and closer when a Southeaster brings high angry waves over the five-foot bank of rocks separating the beach from our front steps.

Oscar and I have been busy with our life inside and outside our little home. Should you come to visit you will find that within these walls there is peace. Each day unfolds by itself. There is no rush to keep to an agenda. Now retired, we have the freedom to follow our own interests. We stop everything to welcome a casual visit from a neighbor. There is a gladness that comes from simple living among folks who have no desire to impress or to be impressed by wealth or background. We dress for warmth, not for looks.

We do keep to one activity in the early morning without fail. Oscar, still in his pajamas, goes into his office/radio shack, fires up his radio and meets with his fellow hams. They are a close group. They know all about one another, the way you do when you visit a friend every day for years. As they age, physical problems take hold. Many have lost their spouses and they have become old and are often lonely. Oscar's radio waves bounce with laughter as stories are told. When bad news is shared, sympathy and offers of help are extended. The hardier ones often travel a hundred miles to assist a buddy.

As Oscar goes to his shack, I go to the piano for my morning devotions. Nothing is planned. I just sing songs that come to mind. They provide the scripture for the day. Hymns of thanksgiving, yearning, understanding and celebration. As I sing, I come awake to the gift of another day in this place.

Oscar tells me that he often leaves the door open so his buddies can hear the hymns. In a sense, we have a little church service going with a congregation all over Minnesota.

In winter, the cabin is warmed by the labor of bodies and willing arms that swing the ax. Our senses delighted by the yeasty smell of freshly baked bread. Simmering soups. Fish sizzling in the frying pan. In summer, we open our doors and windows to let the fresh breezes on the lake flow through the cabin.

When asked where we live, we say, "At the old Severtsen cabin."

But that is only part of the answer. In truth, we live outdoors on this land with the birds, deer, wolves, bear, moose and all of nature. We spend as much time outdoors as we do inside.

Every morning Oscar dons his weathered barn jacket, scoops up some seed and steps outside to give the birds their morning meal. Soon, there is a fluttering of wings as birds of numerous species flock to the table at the top of a tall pole. Among them, families of robins, sparrows, black-capped chickadees, goldfinch, blue Jays, nuthatch. An occasional crimson cardinal.

I like to sit by the kitchen window to watch the show. In winter I crack open the door to hear Oscar singing a dangerously off-key version of *Oh, My Darling Clementine,* while pouring the seed onto the feeder. As if on cue, two or three deer prance out of the woods to gather around the loaded tray. They brush by Oscar, who stands quietly aside, to watch them enjoy their breakfast.

The birds have to wait for a second serving.

The bald eagle nesting in a tall spruce near the house doesn't bother with the bird seed. He goes for the fresh stuff on the lake. He fishes for herring, trout, sturgeon, pike and bass and swoops down on the herring gulls, ducks, mallards and loons who parade near the shore.

In the evening, we sit on the deck to listen to the loons wailing.

One winter night as we sleep, we are awakened by the howling of wolves. They are passing close by, just outside our window. Their cries, pitched high above any human sound, are magnified by what appears to be a pack on the warpath. There, in the safety of our bedroom, I am shaken by terror, as if I am the animal, most likely a deer, that is about to be savaged.

In the morning we walk our property to investigate. The wolves have slaughtered and left remains of several deer.

The blood, red on the white snow.

It is not uncommon to see a black bear sauntering down our driveway, like a neighbor coming to visit. Or a moose licking the salt in the middle of the highway to town. There is power in a 1,500 pound moose—best to stop and wait until he decides to move, however long it takes.

All of these things, they make up the natural world in which we live.

But there is one other thing we see every day that is

more powerful than any wolf, bear or moose.

It is the lake…

We have watched her for two years, but we are by no means close to understanding the many moods of this Lake Superior, the world's largest inland sea. Our ocean.

We do know this. The lake is there. Always there. We greet her every morning at the bedroom window. In the dark of night as we rest, we hear the lake. Often, we slip into a sometimes apprehensive sleep to the beat of a pounding surf. More often, we are lulled by the gentle rhythm of a calm, quiet lapping of waves caressing the shore.

We are aware that Lake Superior is moving. Yes, the lake moves, always it is moving. Even beneath a calm surface Lake Superior moves. In the black hours of night the lake is rising and falling, churning and whirling, moving rocks and boulders that lie hundreds and hundreds of feet below her surface. In winter, beneath thick ice, the lake moves. We hear her move, an eerie sound, the whining of ice against ice, moving upward. Layers of ice tossed skyward to form iridescent mountains of crystal on her surface. Merciless and unstoppable, she moves. Sometimes her anger builds to an uncontrolled rage. I dream of being carried off by a huge wave. Oscar and I hanging on to the pink and yellow roses of our comforter.

At dawn on a summer day, the sun's first glow rouses us. We go from our bed to the lakeside deck. We are called to witness the miracle of the sunrise. Something we will never again take for granted. The lake has become a cathedral like no other in the world. To the east, stained glass windows, layers of deep reds, pinks, oranges and yellows reflect the fires of the rising sun as it travels over the blue waters of the lake. Then, as it happens every morning, catching us by surprise, flooding through our bodies and minds, this overwhelming realization that the lake is so beautiful, so vast, a force so strong even in its most quiet state, that it defies our meager human tools of measurement.

We see God's hand in this place.

And we are made finite.

Two years ago we left the clutter of city life to live quietly, in a cabin by a lake.

Where we saw the sun rise.

27.

THE STORM

1994. THE YEAR BEGINS with a long, frigid winter, one snowstorm after another. Minnesota's far north eases into spring slowly. One day in April the thermometer outside our cabin door teases us with a temperature in the high 30s. A virtual heat wave. We can feel our bones beginning to thaw. By mid-morning every kid in the nearby town of Grand Marais is bouncing about in shorts. But, the moment we observe that spring is here at last, the mercury plunges down well below freezing. This perverse game of yo-yo goes on throughout April and May. When we begin to rejoice in warm spring rains, sleet or snow sends shivers through both spine and spirit.

But June does come! Sweet summer days bright with the sun's golden warmth, long leisurely hours under pastel skies, frogs partying noisily in our pond as Mother Mallard disapprovingly shepherds her brood to a more genteel neighborhood.

This is the first time we have experienced summer up here, although we have lived in the brown cedar cabin beside Lake Superior for two previous very cold and wet seasons folks told us were called summer. We are able to garden, relishing the freedom of short sleeves. Oscar and I design a wildflower garden to reinforce the pleasure we feel throughout the summer as one variety after another unfolds its own special beauty along the roadsides and in the woods.

The lake becomes serene, allowing us to venture out in the canoe. Peering down into the crystal water, we see huge rocks washed round by centuries of pounding water, giant parents of the small many colored stones we find on our cobblestone beach. We paddle west to our neighbor's log house where a massive rock ledge extends out beneath the glassy surface of the lake. This pre-Cambrian volcanic outflow was smoothed by glacial scraping during the most recent ice age.

Our cabin and the cabins along the shore seem so small in the face of such power.

The halcyon days stretch on into September. We sigh as we split and stack our eight cords of wood for the winter ahead. Then autumn gently begins to announce itself. First, the low lying red stems and sumac change from summer's green to a deep crimson, the swamp maples to a burnt burgundy. Toward the middle of the month the sugar maples on Maple Hill burst into a glorious rusty red. The birches and aspen pass from gold to lemon, yellows made brilliant by the dark green hues of spruce and balsam.

Flocks of snow buntings gather in our driveway, signaling the summer people to close their cabins for yet another winter.

Oscar rushes out to scatter millet, hoping to tempt these joyful brown and white creatures to linger with us before they migrate further south.

The Bethlehem Lutheran Church Book Club takes advantage of the mild weather to drive 40 miles up the lake shore to the log home of Lars and Tina Lindahl. When Lars and Tina refurbished her Grandfather Quist's one room house on the lake a decade ago, they decided not to bother with indoor plumbing.

Lars, a retired Lutheran minister, placed the bathtub outside in front of the house overlooking the lake. Tina thought this was a bit strange, but it sure made it easier to fill the tub. A water tank with a wood burning furnace beneath it completed the system.

On this particular Tuesday morning Lars is enjoying a morning bath, taking a bit longer than usual to watch the seagulls dip for herring just off shore. About this time the ladies of the book club are processing down the mile long road from the highway to the Lindahl's.

Tina is in the kitchen at the cook stove dipping *fattigmann* dough into hot oil. At the sound of the first car she hears Lars yelling something unintelligible as he takes a flying leap out of the tub and scurries around the back corner of the house.

"Thank you, Lord, for good September weather for bathing. And for good ears in our old age," she murmurs.

"And please keep warming the day while Lars hides in the outhouse," she adds.

Although October has come, we are still soothed by balmy days. Now the mountain ash begin to brighten. Abundant clusters of orange-red berries drip from the spindly branches of these shrub-like gray green trees that have stood so plain and invisible for years. The woods glow with red jewels everywhere. Old Swede tells us that he has never seen the mountain ash so flamboyant. By November the berries have mellowed like old wine. The richly burnished bunches are topped with tiny white bonnets of snow as they hang merrily from the branches.

But something is off with this warm weather and so little snow. The summer-like peaceful beauty belies something menacing in the air.

The unusually warm autumn weather continues into

Thanksgiving week. We journey down to Minneapolis for a family Thanksgiving, but return home before the weekend is over. Good planning! Sunday morning we awake to a winter storm warning. Angry waves are crashing onto the shore of the lake. Oscar ominously notes that the wind is from the northeast. We stay home from church to keep an eye on the lake. Wind gusts howl through the bending trees under a dark gray sky. Steadily building waves lash across our beach and over the bank near our cabin. By two in the afternoon we are seeing trees falling, some close to the house and outbuildings. A giant root erupts in our neighbor's woods, alerting us to the loss of a towering spruce. We watch in horror as several birches that have stood for 80 years on the lake side of the cabin are uprooted by wind and wave. They fall in slow motion into the sea.

About three o'clock it begins to snow heavily. By five Oscar is out on the bank, barely visible in the swirling snow as he tries to save our beach steps. Several dead trees have been thrown with unbelievable power against the wooden steps, smashing them and loosening them from their moorings. The surging lake threatens to swallow him. Somehow he manages to lasso the steps and tie them to the front deck. At 11 p.m. we reluctantly decide to go to bed, although the storm does not seem to be abating.

The first light of morning brings a surprising white peace and quiet. Over a foot of snow covers the fallen trees scattered about the yard. We see that a large spruce went down near the kitchen window during the night. Beside it, blood red against the snow, a cardinal digs for sunflower seeds, while above on the feeder, chickadees and nuthatches snatch a seed or two before a red squirrel chases them away. A large area of beach gravel and debris on the lakeside of the cabin tells us that while we slept huge waves came up to the foundation wall.

By late morning we are plowed and shoveled. We drive our neighbor, Carol, to town to survey the damage. Grand Marais has been hard hit by the storm. Waves, two stories high, have rolled over the seawall at the foot of Main Street, causing it to break and flood the entire business district. Several streets are now skating rinks. We learn that surprised diners in the East Bay Hotel escaped as waist high water crashed through the windows. Scattered boulders, smashed picnic tables and mountains of silt rise out of the snowbanks on Coast Guard Point. Now we understand what the French fur traders meant when they named the town Grand Marais—Big Pond. Periodically, the lake comes in to reclaim the swampland that was filled in years ago for the building of downtown Grand Marais.

The town is filled with people, all pitching in to remove fallen trees, to board up broken windows and doors and to clean up the water and gravel mess. Christmas is around the corner and we all need one another in the aftermath of the storm.

Carol, Oscar and I trek through the snow and debris to her antique shop, located on the East Bay. We follow Carol to the front porch. It isn't there. We move to the front door. Gone. Stepping into the store, we see that the lake had thrown the door across the showroom, burying it in six inches of gravel, strewing glass antiques and furniture everywhere. A quiet belies the fury of the night. Ice encases all. We cannot pry the precious antiques from the floor.

Feeling that we must do something, we decide to reinstall the door. After wedging the door into the opening, Oscar turns to pick up a screwdriver. At that moment, a young deputy sheriff, eager to apprehend reported looters, opens the unfastened door in SWAT team fashion, sending it crashing to the floor, breaking the glass panes at the top.

Oscar, always keen on propriety, introduces our trio to a now ashen-faced young man, who, after a moment of silence, realizes we are not the bad guys.

The storm has passed. Night comes again with bright stars in a clear sky. We do not know what the darkness will bring. But some reflection on the past year, with its seasons of dark and light, cold and warmth, the sometimes overwhelming challenges and the abiding harmony they have brought us, leads us to a newfound fear for the terrible power of nature and God.

28.
WHAT WOULD
OSCAR DO?

1999. IT IS MIDNIGHT in our cabin on Lake Superior. I am alone in Oscar's ham shack listening to one of his many radios. A cry comes over the radio waves.

"The fire is spreading, heading in your direction!" the voice yells, "Put Sanden in a shelter!"

"All of you, in a shelter!"

A fire shelter. An aluminum tent that is the last resort if you can't outrun a fire. My heart sinks. I grasp the radio, hold it close to my chest, as I would do my husband if I were with him. Oscar is a member of our town's emergency management team. He offers his ham radio as a means of communicating in a disaster. On this quiet summer evening, while Oscar tunes his radios, he hears that there is a massive fire in the nearby Boundary Waters of Northern Minnesota. The Boundary Waters Wilderness Area lies within the Superior National Forest, an area well over a million acres. A mix of forest, lakes and streams.

The forest rangers at the fire line are in trouble. Their radio is not working. They lose contact with the air tanker pilot, who awaits vital information from the ground crew about the location of the fire. The hot spots. Once he receives it, he will drop his load of water directly on the fire and the hot spots.

"I can fix it," Oscar shouts, as he packs his radio, rushes out to the car, breaks the speed limit on a 25-mile drive deep into the woods—to the fire line.

Back home, I have been listening to a radio in his ham shack, following him through the long hours of the night. Oscar, on arrival, with his radio, immediately establishes communications with the air tanker.

Then, at midnight, comes the terrifying news.

Oscar and the rangers are in imminent danger.

I wait for what seems an eternity. Praying, standing there in his radio shack.

As the rangers prepare the tents, Oscar makes radio contact with the pilot of the air tanker. Who scores a perfect hit on the approaching fire. The rangers and their volunteer radio man are safe. Oscar is sent home.

In addition to his radios, Oscar always has his toolbox handy. He solves less hazardous problems for our neighbors. They know who to call before they call the plumber or the electrician. Oscar can fix it.

Oscar and I share a hunger for music. He is the audio man for the choral groups I help organize and direct. Together we fill the silence of our home and car with music. Sacred music. Classical music. Operatic voices. A mix of popular music thrown in.

He smiles when I sing Grieg's Norwegian songs.

Our best date is a night at the symphony. One evening, as delighted as I am to watch a heavy snow falling outside the windows of our snug, warm cabin, I begin to feel trapped. There has been one snowstorm after another for the past month. We have been cooped up for too long. Our roads are reduced to narrow paths, running between high walls of icy-hard snow. And now there is more coming down.

"We're going to miss the symphony," I lament. "Why can't we just get in the Explorer and drive slowly?"

I am on the verge of tears. Oscar hates to see me cry. So he drives me north over the Canadian border in a raging snow storm. I scream when we spin into a mountain of snow while attempting to park our car. We shuffle through the blinding snow, over what seems to be an acre of black ice, to the entrance of the Thunder Bay Symphony Hall. A Finnish violinist plays Vivaldi's *Four Seasons*. We float through the sweet music of Spring, the warmth of Summer, the spicy perfume of Autumn. We nod knowingly at the moods of Winter.

As we leave the hall, the snow falls quietly.

Oscar always knows what to do to bring a smile to his wife's face.

＊ ＊ ＊

2001. After 10 years, we leave our cabin on the shore of Lake Superior to live in the New England countryside. We need to be close to our grandchildren.

It has been over 20 years since his stroke. He was a younger man then, at forty-eight, and is now approaching his seventieth birthday. His left side, the hand, arm and leg, are still weak. He relies on his right side, which has become remarkably strong. When folks notice his characteristic limp, he tells them it is due to an old football injury.

Here he is, misbehaving. I close my eyes. Look the other

way. My husband, who does not look upon himself as disabled, is climbing up a ladder to the roof of our Dublin, New Hampshire house. Oscar is installing his ham radio antenna. When he comes down—in one piece, I hope—he will lie on his back to fix the plumbing under the sink. I stand by to help him get back on his feet. Steady him as he walks.

Against my wishes, he tries to ride his old bike. He falls, but has no serious injuries. He drives a snowmobile on a frozen lake. I come away with a broken wrist. Seeing his grin as he revs the engine is worth the penalty I have to pay.

We take daily walks. His balance is bad. There is a good chance he will fall if he forgets his cane. He does not complain. I do see his eyes, wistful, at the sight of a jogger flying by. In that moment, my heart aches for him.

We are at a town meeting. Tempers are rising as the residents debate the pros and cons of acquiring a badly-needed truck for the town dump. The argument seems to be at an impasse. I reach over to poke Oscar in the chest.

I whisper, "Speak."

Oscar struggles to his feet. The crowd grows quiet as his voice rises, calming the fires and bringing resolution. This happens often at meetings.

A poke in the chest. He speaks. Problem resolved. After his death, a friend thought of getting a new license plate: WWOD (What Would Oscar Do?)

* * *

Oscar solves problems in numerous ways. By acting quickly or simply by listening. He is a father who never sets down rules. Never preaches. Instead, he listens to our children. His love, trust, and respect speaks to them where words fail.

Armed with these tools, they work out the solutions to their problems. Our children admire and love their dad. They model their lives after him. There is this unspoken expectation that they will always do their best. They see in their father the resources of an inner power that can be called upon in times of trouble. He is quietly proud of his three children, who grow into an early independence. Choosing their own paths. And yet, always, he is the dad who listens, who is there for his kids.

I enjoy watching Oscar interact with young children. During gatherings, he takes time to sit down with the little ones.

It is a Sunday morning in Dublin. Pastor Mike is preaching. A toddler in the front pew gets restless. He breaks loose from his mother's arms, races down the aisle to the back of the church. Climbs up on Grandpa Oscar's lap for a whispered talk. Plays with his cane.

Teenagers have always had a special place in our hearts. As a young couple, we led the youth groups at several churches. Some 20 teens filled the front pews at Erik's baptism. Erik's godparents were in their teens.

I remember Oscar, some years ago, sitting in his home office, listening to a distraught boy. Kyle was a neighbor, the son of an alcoholic father. At fifteen, Kyle was going to run away. Oscar listened to Kyle's story. He gently brought Kyle to an understanding of what would happen if he ran away. Kyle went home stronger. He had a friend across the street.

Our work with teenagers opened our ears to the music of John Lennon and Paul McCartney.

Hey Jude, don't make it bad. Take a sad song

and make it better.

This was Oscar's message to Kyle.

* * *

1990. Our son, Paul, phones our home in Glendale from his Navy base in Maine to ask us to find Tammy and keep her safe. We have never met Tammy. She is seventeen, the sister of Paul's friend, a fellow pilot. Tammy, a singer, has come to Hollywood from Florida with hopes of getting discovered. Her girlfriend has gone back home, leaving her alone in a one room apartment. No furniture but a mattress. No money. She has a clerking job at the Galleria. A stranger approaches her. He promises her a modeling job, invites her to come to his studio for photos. And, by the way, does she do lingerie? Tammy is going to see him tomorrow.

Of course she will tell him she doesn't do lingerie…

Paul gives me a description of Tammy. I grab my car keys, and am on my way!

Paul and I have lived long enough with Oscar to know that when you see a problem you must act quickly.

Tammy stays with us that night and for the next three months. Oscar and I come to know and love Tammy as a daughter. We are privileged to give her the space and time she needs to find a direction for her life. Tammy cooks and cleans with me. She meets our friends, provides our family with an excuse to take sight-seeing drives around Los Angeles. She sings with me in our church choir. Gets a job in a church office. Tammy comes into our lives when our house is too quiet. Laura and Paul are married and living on the east coast. Erik is soon to leave for college. Tammy brings new life into our home. The decision to return home to Florida and to attend college comes slowly. But we are not in a hurry to lose the company of this beautiful young woman.

Somewhere in a box of old letters, there is a letter from Tammy:

You took me in. You saved me.

No, Tammy, I think. We just loved you.

* * *

Oscar liked an afternoon nap. He solved problems during his power naps. I can't remember the issue, but I do recall the anxiety of one terrible day. I see him standing silent, listening to my cries of frustration. Then, without a word, he turns around and leaves the room. I next see him sitting up after a good sleep. He walks over to me, envelopes my hands in his big, capable ones. No problem, however huge, will survive the power of those hands.

When I look up, I see a light in his hazel eyes.

"This is what we'll do," he says.

What would Oscar do?

Over a decade has passed since his death. Still, I ask myself this question almost daily, as I struggle to manage life without him. A life without him? No. He is still alive in my memory and in the memory of his children and the hundreds of others whose lives he touched.

In my memory I see him as a young man, an old man, a husband, father, naval officer and best friend.

I see him as a gentleman.

I see him as a man of great energy, who uses his keen mind and strength to make the world a better place.

I see him as a rock to cling to when the world is in shatters.

I see him as a teacher. He teaches me that life can be full and rich, life can be glorious, even in the face of overwhelming limitations.

He teaches me how to love. Real love is something that not only demands, but welcomes, the gift of oneself.

In that love, Oscar and I, together, have a deep and lasting happiness. Our love will never die. He will never leave me.

I often find myself asking him what he would do if…

I am visiting with my friend, Anne, in her apartment. Anne's husband passed away years ago. Anne points to a life-size bust, head and neck, of a handsome man. It rests on a table in her living room.

He looks like he is ready to speak.

"This is my husband, Harry."

I nod, as if to greet him.

Anne walks over to pat his head.

"I talk to him every day."

29.

WIDOW

OSCAR PASSED AWAY several weeks ago after a courageous battle with cancer. Family and friends fill our home with the noises of the living while we work feverishly together to prepare a proper farewell to my beloved husband. Our three grown children and the grandchildren are here. There is no time to grieve. So many of our loved ones have traveled from distant places to say goodbye to him. The memorial service is planned swiftly so that they can attend and return to their lives.

Now, the service is a thing of the past. My family and close friends have departed, taking their robust sounds, their energy, with them.

I wave goodbye to the last of them. I enter the condo to a blast of silence. The air is dead, a vacuum has sucked out the sound. I can barely breathe in the stillness. There is a vacancy that I am too exhausted to fill. The absence of sound is malevolent.

I am alone. For the first time.

I awake in the morning. Half asleep, I reach for him beside me. It comes as a painful shock, the reality that he isn't here. I look for the morning chatter of two people still in love after almost 60 years of marriage, and there is nothing but silence.

I sit next to an empty chair at the breakfast table. I tell

myself that this is the way it is to be.

And I let go of the tears I have so bravely held back during the days I needed to be strong, in control of the painful decisions that come with losing a spouse.

So this is how it is to be, I say to myself as I escape to the shelter of my bed. Where I sleep fitfully, awaking often to a persistent replay of the days and hours that Oscar lay dying. Guilt raises its ugly head, a venomous snake that won't let go as it wraps its steely arms around my neck.

Why did I leave Oscar's side on that last night when he was struggling to breathe? The children were standing vigil all that long night. They insisted I get some rest. True, I was drained, dead on my feet, after many sleepless nights watching him slowly fade. I was like a robot, letting them lead me to bed.

Knowing that I awoke to be at his side during his final moments did nothing to assuage my guilt. Why, oh why wasn't I with him for every precious moment of his last hours?

Why didn't I get him to the doctors earlier, when he complained of feeling tired? Maybe he would have been saved.

Why did I leave him to go to choir practice, to Sunday church, when he was undergoing the pain of chemotherapy?

I am ridden by guilt. Unable to forgive myself.

The memorial service was filled with Oscar's favorite hymns and classical sacred music. The choir sang a beautiful arrangement of Handel's "Largo."

Now, at home, I talk to God. In some twisted way I am tortured by the belief that I was in some way responsible for Oscar's pain. I pray for God's assurance that he is at last at peace.

I phone our insurance company and I am put on hold. I try to compose myself. I will have to speak aloud the painful words, *my husband has passed away.* I hold the phone to my ear. An orchestra with solo violin begins to play. I sit in astonishment. I am hearing Handel's *Largo* in all its glory.

I am not alone in this. God is with me!

"Don't do anything you don't want to do," says my friend, Pat, a psychiatric social worker.

She knows well that I need to move through a time of grief and acceptance before I will be ready to reach out and begin a new life as a widow.

When the leftovers in the refrigerator expire, I take a trip to the market for some groceries. There, among the fruits and vegetables, I see a bag of figs. I hold it in my hands, tears streaming down my face. An elderly woman touches my arm.

"Are you alright, dear?" she says.

"Yes," I choke, "It's just—that—my—husband—loved—figs." And I sob while a stranger holds me in her arms.

I return to our church a different person. I am marked by sadness. My heart is weighed down by a heavy darkness. I carry a river of tears inside me. It overflows in an instant; my emotions are beyond control. I sit in the back pew—Oscar's pew. Arms reach out to comfort me as I weep through the singing of the hymns.

A car approaches as I drive up the hill toward home. An old gentleman is driving, his wife sits beside him. She is frowning, as if terribly bored. She should be celebrating! Her husband is alive.

I am filled with envy. A nasty feeling. I must try to focus on the time Oscar and I had together.

It is the little things that shatter me. The machines that run the home have no respect for the moods and competency of the inhabitants. They go to war with me. The refrigerator stops working. The garage door won't open, and the car sits, useless, inside.

I am alone and helpless. I cry in frustration.

My grandson, Cameron, is eleven. I pick him up after school. Bring him home to hear about his day while we share some chocolate chip cookies. Cam is a good listener. Sometimes I forget he is just a kid. I start to tell a story about his Grandpa. My grief is raw, just weeks after his passing. Suddenly, I am overcome. Cam, tears falling, reaches out to hold me in a hug. Then, he lets go and runs out of the kitchen. Returns with Mango, the dog. Envelopes the three of us in a group hug.

You are never alone when there is a child and a dog to hug.

Erik, my son, and his partner, Saleta, take me to Spain, to Galicia, where we tour the Atlantic coast. We stop at a tiny boutique hotel, settle in adjacent rooms. I have been a restless sleeper since Oscar's death. In the quiet of my bed I am haunted by my loss. I often dream of Oscar, mostly pleasant dreams, but in some of them Oscar is in danger and I cannot help him. I read a travel book late into the night. Then fall asleep. I wake up, screaming, after a horrible nightmare. Erik rushes in, soothes me, lies by my side until dawn.

My strength and peace of mind returned gradually, week by week. I look on that time of healing with gratitude to my loving God, my precious family and the friends and strangers who upheld me when I was sinking.

I cannot name the exact morning that I looked in the mirror and found the old Me. Smiling. A calm, a serenity, had washed over me as I awakened. I felt the old eagerness to greet the day and to make the most of it.

I wasn't sure what I was going to do with my life as a widow. But, Mama had taught me well. She lived kindness in her beautiful smile, her soft voice and warm embrace of friends and strangers. She met life shattering blows with grace and resilience. Mama skipped over minor troubles like a child jumping over a puddle. She was the most cheerful person I ever met.

Mama's positive outlook was deeply embedded in my heart. I knew that there was a new, exciting life out there, waiting for me.

All I needed to do was wait to see it happen. And while I waited, there were bright memories to warm me...

He told these stories many times around the table
as the family gathered for dinner,
or when company came.
His mind was quick, his memory for details, amazing.
He would sit in silence, listening to the others
talk about whatever came to mind.
Then, just when we began to wonder at his quiet,
he began a story.
And we would sit in silence and listen
to that magnificent voice
to that gifted storyteller
as he held us in suspense
as we waited for the end of the story.

We loved them all,
but each of us had our favorites.
The story of how his preacher father
held him safe in his strong arms,

kept him from blowing away
in the wind of the Texas hurricane of 1933.
The story of how the Sanden family
came from Sweden, via Oslo,
bringing their faith, music, and artistry
to Evanston, Illinois where a traveler stopped
at Grandfather Oscar's upholstery shop in the early 1900s,
helping out in exchange for a few day's room and board.
A young fellow, played his guitar, recited his poetry.
Name was Carl Sandburg.
Then, to a lumber town in Louisiana
where the church folk would gather Sunday nights
at Grandpa and Grandma Sanden's farmhouse,
Aunt Dagny at the organ for a hymn sing,
the table loaded with Swedish meatballs, potatoes, gravy,
whipped cream atop fruit pies, marzipan layered cakes.
Aunts Mathilda and Dagmar loudly urging
young Oscar and his tiny brother
"Go ahead, don't you like my cake? Have some more!"

Later, the boys would roll in the grass out back by the
outhouse, clutching their stomachs. Groaning.

The story of a tall, skinny fifteen year old
in Levis and cowboy boots, fresh from the rural South
found himself up North caught in the whirlwind
of a huge Minneapolis high school.
Senior year, they said can't, he said cain't.

A college freshman at sixteen, too thin for the Navy,

stuffed himself with bananas and milkshakes for a month,
didn't gain an ounce, but true grit got him into the
NROTC.

The story of how a young ensign,
unable to leave his ship at sea,
mailed an engagement ring to his parents,
his mom taking the streetcar all the way
across Minneapolis on Valentines Day 1954.
Asked Lila to do her the honor of marrying her son.
Stories of storms at sea, whales bouncing around the ship,
picking up downed pilots in the Gulf of Tonkin
where a helicopter hovering high over the ship,
lowered Commander Sanden and his briefcase
on a rope with orders to assume command.
Carrying a live explosive, wires hanging out,
from a jammed gun mount,
throwing it over the side of the ship.

Sporting a digger hat on the bridge of the ship after
losing a game of Acey-Duecey to the mayor of Brisbane.
Seeing JFK alight from a helicopter, all smiles,
at Annapolis, while Middies cheered.
Our president was shot two weeks later.

So many stories, yet untold.
But now, as it must come to all,
our storyteller has journeyed on.

No more stories, but one he lived, ours to tell.

A story of endurance, good cheer, in the face of years of pain.
A story of humble thankfulness for a cup half full.
A story of family, faith, of love, and hope.
His gentle spirit departing as he sang, off key,
the family bedtime song,
I love you, a bushel and a peck
whispered in my ear
I love you, Sweetie Pie.

30.
WITH A SONG
IN MY HEART

2016. WHEN I FIRST walk into the apartment in Altadena, I am
struck by the bright light, golden sunshine against an azure sky,
entering the space from three walls of tall windows. Windows
that stretch from near the floor to the high ceiling.

I know that I will be happy here, living in the light.

I am eighty-three years young. It is here, at a place called
MonteCedro, that I plan to live out my days. MonteCedro–
meaning mountain of cedars–sits below the wooded foothills
of the San Gabriel Mountains in northern Los Angeles county.
Its doors have just opened; its mission is to provide a healthy,
active and fulfilling life for its 200 residents. It serves up a
menu of educational, cultural, and recreational offerings from
outside resources and from the residents, who bring a wealth of
knowledge and experience to the community.

On this first morning I step into the shower with a
prayer of thanks for this beautiful new home. As I relax under
the warm water, I begin to sing. Singing is as much a part of
my daily shower as the water and the soap. Today it is an aria
from Mozart's *Marriage of Figaro–Voi Che Sapeta*. This is how
I celebrate each day: with a song.

I have always loved choral music. I read music and harmonized with my sister while I was still in primary school. I have studied voice and been a choir member for most of my life.

A small group of my fellow residents and I form a choir. We need a director. I am not a professional director, but have directed small groups. I agree to act as temporary director. Together, we begin a journey with many challenges. Over half our core group have never sung in a choir. Many cannot read music. However, the only requirement is that you like to sing. I take a poll. Most are shower singers. A good sign. All residents are invited to join our Monday afternoon rehearsals.

In the next few months we grow a choir, we grow an audience, and we raise spirits.

Five years later, I am still directing the choir, having gone through some on the job training. Over 30 singers have joined me on this journey. We are a family, working together to create something beautiful.

One of our singers, Mary, brought her husband, Bruce, to choir practice. Bruce had suffered a stroke. He hadn't spoken a word in months. He began to attend rehearsals regularly. He did not sing or utter a word, or give any indication that he was enjoying the music.

Then, one day, Bruce began to sing along with the choir. Music works miracles.

Caregivers begin to bring their patients to choir rehearsal. David and others like him have suffered memory loss. But they remember all the songs of the past, and sing them with gusto.

Lillian is not happy at MonteCedro. She does not make friends. She rarely smiles. She walks down the halls, lost in a pool of sadness.

"Why did I leave my lovely home? Come here to live? I have no life in this place. I might as well be dead."

Several choir members invite Lillian to come to a choir rehearsal. Lillian comes alive when she hears the music. It becomes a part of her, fills her. It seems to flow through her, from the tips of her toes to the top of her head. Her body dances with the waves of the sound. She raises her voice in response. And is happy.

Lillian has found her joy.

And so have I.

EPILOGUE

2023

My Dearest Oscar,

I have seen your smile, your tears, as I write this memory of my life, your life, and our life together. I feel your presence in the hours, days, and months of isolation the Pandemic has imposed upon our world. I have dedicated them to meditating about our lives, woven together in the lives of so many.

I have heard your voice encouraging me, as I concentrate upon sweeping my mind clear. Opening it to the voices of the past. And the present.

And then to write honestly.

A soft breeze dances on the California sunshine that streams through the open window beside my desk. I feel you are sitting beside me. Warming me.

I close my eyes to better hear you calling.

"Lila...Lila...Lila..."

And I feel like a princess.

Farewell, My Prince,
Lila

AFTERWORD

IF, OR SHOULD I say when, the big earthquake, flood, or fire comes, these are the things I will grab as I run to safety: my coffee pot, as many books as I can carry, my choir music and my *sisu*.

I grew up Finnish. Finns are great readers. What else is there to do when the winter days are as dark as night? And you're not always sure if it's day or night? Finns are in need of rich coffee to zap them awake while they are reading all those books. I did not grow up in Finland, but my grandparents did. Coffee is in my genes. And books. Stacks of books waiting to be read.

I would be lost without my choir music. Six years ago, I came to Altadena to live a quiet life in retirement. I soon realized that life doesn't stop when you enter your eighties. Nor does your passion, your hunger, for the things that have made you happy. In my case, to be a part of a choir that makes music come alive.

This is why I love our choir. This is why I safeguard the music.

There is one last thing I will carry. It is invisible; yet it is the most important survival tool a Finn can own. It is *sisu*. The Finnish word for a determination to overcome. *Sisu* is a mindset. A resolution to take life by the tail, to master it and enjoy it. A resolve that must be renewed every morning as you awake.

I never thought I would have what it takes to dedicate

myself to writing a book from start to finish. But, the pandemic gave me the time and my Finnish *sisu*, the resolve.

Above all I thank Loren Kantor, writer and teacher extraordinaire, who had me read my chapters to his writing class. This book would not exist without his generous and careful consideration and encouragement. Thanks to my journalist brother, Allan Hietala, who, at ninety-two is also writing his memoirs, and to my son, teacher, writer, composer Erik Sanden. Both carried me through the drafts from the beginning to the end. Thanks to all who so kindly read the drafts of this book. Thanks to the support of my family and friends, those not mentioned. I carry them in my heart forever. And finally, special thanks to Mick and Diane Prodger of Elm Grove Publishing who took my manuscript and made it into the book you now have in hand.

Lila

Lila Hietala Sanden

www.ingramcontent.com/pod-product-compliance
Lightning Source LLC
Chambersburg PA
CBHW071324120626
46546CB00002B/424